Music and Vital Congregations

Music and Vital Congregations

A Practical Guide for Clergy

WILLIAM BRADLEY ROBERTS

Church Publishing
NEW YORK

Cover design by Brenda Klinger
Interior design and typesetting by Beth Oberholtzer

Library of Congress Cataloging-in-Publication Data

Roberts, William Bradley.
    Music and vital congregations : a practical guide for clergy /
by William Bradley Roberts.
        p.   cm.
    Includes bibliographical references.
    ISBN 978-0-89869-623-3 (pbk.)
    1. Music in churches. I. Title.
ML3001.R63 2009
264'.2—dc22

                                                            2009015135

Church Publishing, Incorporated.
445 Fifth Avenue
New York, New York 10016
www.churchpublishing.org

5 4 3 2 1

This book is dedicated with gratitude
to the clergy under whose supervision I have served
as a church musician. In chronological order they are:
Joe, Orville, Bill, J. P., Andrew,
Frank, John H., John A., Gil,
David, Roger, John K., and Luis

Contents

Acknowledgments

Books are seldom written without assistance, and this one is no exception. Joanna Bowen Gillespie was a patient, thorough, and painstaking reader, and this volume bears the marks of her life-long experience with church music, as well as her expertise as a scholarly and articulate writer of history. Mary Lonsdale Baker shared her insight as a professional musician and a teacher of English. Marilyn Haskel, editor at Church Publishing, Inc., voiced her encouragement and imparted her wisdom as a seasoned church musician. David W. Hoover, as always, generously contributed the love, friendship, and faith that lend joy to life.

Introduction

Deep river,
my home is over Jordan;
Deep river,
I want to cross over into campground.[1]

Music and the Holy

Music is integral to worship. It sets the tone of worship more than any other aspect. Our identity as a people—what our values are, our culture, our theology, our mission—is often signaled to people by music before they ever hear it described in words. Much of our worship is word-oriented, and Christianity needs its rational, discursive presentation. What people in our culture seem to crave, however, is a sense of wonder, mystery, holiness, transcendence. For those churches who value liturgy, even the words alone, of course, can carry a sense of transcendence, but music can undergird, amplify, illuminate the language of praise and prayer. Music gives wings to worship.

I gained a flash of insight from an incident that happened in a church I served on the East Coast. The young adult group decided that it needed a worship service during the week. Their traveling on weekends (or partying) made Sunday morning an inconvenient time for worship. They also felt that their service needed to have its own particular flavor. I was not involved in the initial meetings, and so when word reached me that they wanted a different kind of music than we ordinarily offered on Sunday mornings, I confess that I was nervous. What were they going to ask for? Would our church's music resources be able to handle it? Did I have the ability to help them create this new kind of music?

Nothing could have surprised me more than the exact request they made. They wanted a service of *a capella* (unaccompanied; voices alone) music. It was the exact opposite of what I expected, which was something extroverted and rhythmic, perhaps with guitars and drums. These were bright, young, well-educated Washingtonians, some with demanding jobs in ambitious careers. Yet what they most needed in their lives was the numinous.

A few weeks later I phoned a colleague on the West Coast, preparing to speak there at a music and liturgy conference. We chatted about various goings-on in our respective parishes, when he shared the following story with me: The young adults in his church had also convened to discuss a new service with content and character that addressed their needs. With amazement in his voice, he stammered, "You're not going to believe what they asked for." Thinking back on my own parish's young adults, I chuckled, "I might. Try me." He continued, "They want a medieval liturgy."

Who among my generation would ever have predicted such a request? These young adults, on both coasts, were longing for something deeply interior. They wanted an encounter with God, with mystery, and they felt that music could create the conditions leading toward that journey.

Not all young adults would agree with the two groups described above. But whatever the quality of worship we are called to create, music is the strongest single factor. It expresses the inexpressible, gives voice to the unspeakable, awakens the spirit to God's presence, and unites disparate people; it challenges our identity, calls us outside ourselves, raises our spirits, and lifts us to the throne of grace. Music gives wings to worship.

Missing from Theological Training

At a recent ecumenical meeting of clergy and musicians, an African American Baptist pastor pronounced, "Just give them great preaching and great music, and they'll come." It's a simple formula with a lot of truth to it. Preaching and music, when they are powerful, draw people to worship, and, perhaps more critical, bring them back again and again. I don't mean to imply that music and preaching are the only important things about church, or even that they are superior to other aspects of parish life. Liturgy, Christian education, outreach, service, pastoral care, mission and evangelism— all are crucial in an effective parish. Yet music and preaching are so public that everyone who comes to church responds to them.

Clergy are trained in preaching—homiletics being one discipline every seminarian has to study. Music, on the other hand, is often given short shrift in theological training—a large number of schools, in fact, require no instruction in music at all. This is especially tragic for the many seminarians who are new converts to the faith, or who have changed denominations. They are likely to enter parish ministry with no understanding of the specific music tradition they will represent. They will not fully know the culture they are about to enter unless they have encountered its music. Even those students who are lifelong members of their denomination may have grown up with little knowledge of its music tradition.

If the African American Baptist pastor was right, then half of what attracts and holds people at a church is being overlooked in theological education. Even though pastors will seldom have direct responsibility for the music ministry, they are likely to hire and supervise those who do. They will also influence the selection of music in the process of worship planning. No one, apart from the Holy Spirit, has as much influence over a music ministry—its style, how important a parish regards it, and who leads and develops it.

Why the Lack of Training?

Given the importance of music in worship, why then the paucity of music in seminary curricula? First of all, academic deans in seminaries are besieged with demands to add this course or that to the academic catalog. In each case, the faculty member believes that the course she or he requests is essential for clergy education. At the same time members of the faculty feel strongly that their particular discipline is not given enough time in the schedule, and that students will leave the institution unprepared in that critical area. In smaller schools the music professor often doesn't have a seat at the table when this discussion occurs, because she or he is probably adjunct or part-time. Therefore, music faculty, having limited involvement with campus process, exert little influence.

In a larger context, the absence of music instruction is symptomatic of our culture's emphasis on the practical and the economic. Art is seldom practical or economical. Mathematics and science are easier to measure in our values because they immediately benefit our commerce and industry. To be sure, art deepens and enriches our lives, but in ways not numerically demonstrated. Its effects are interior. Much of Christian life, however, *is* interior, evoking our natural affinity for art.

The Power of Beauty

"Beauty will save the world." So says Dostoevsky in his novel *The Idiot*.[2] Upon first hearing, this may sound heretical to Christians, since salvation is God's redeeming work through Christ. Even to the non-Christian, however, such a bold proclamation may seem naïve or foolish. How, in the face of the yawning needs of our world, can beauty have any concrete strength, much less save us?

In his Nobel Lecture (1970), Alexandr Solzhenitsyn tried to explain Dostoevsky's comment. "Those works of art which have scooped up the truth and presented it to us as a living force—they take hold of us, compel us, and nobody ever, not even in the ages to come, will appear to refute them." It is "vain to reiterate what does not reach the heart."[3]

Jesus the artist used parable to convey truths to the heart. Their often-enigmatic beauty draws us into them. We are caught up in the power of the stories, each a miniature work of art, and we see ourselves, our world, and, ultimately, the nature of God more clearly. If God is the essence of beauty, then anything of beauty is a metaphor for the divine. Beauty in this sense is essential to life; it points toward God. Our society's preference for consumerism and materialism can't negate the power of art. Christians, of all people, will understand, and insist upon, the inclusion of art in our public life, and especially in the church.

Of course, music poorly performed will make little contribution to people's lives; indeed, in the parish it will detract from the effectiveness of worship. Not every church is able to produce music of the highest quality in its services, but every church can use the resources God has given them to create the very best they are able. British-American theologian and musician Erik Routley (1917–1982) made this statement in attempting to summarize the music philosophy of Charles Wesley: "Give us the best music we can have, but make it *friendly* to the people."[4] It is the best succinct philosophy of church music I know.

Throughout history, music and the other arts have been an intrinsic element of liturgy. Music at its best ushers us into the holy, deepens our prayers, heightens our praise, provides an aura of beauty that reflects the nature of God, lifts us into God's presence, and strengthens our bonds with all creation. Clergy who have experienced this power are likely to insist upon it in the local parishes they lead.

The Occasion for This Book

For the past two years I have had the rare privilege of teaching in a seminary that does value music in the church. Here I have had the joy of engaging with bright and energetic students on many of the themes in this book. Often they focused my attention on matters that I might've otherwise overlooked. They brought perspectives that were different from mine, and I was the recipient of their broadening insights. To my utter consternation God insists upon teaching me things while I am standing before a crowd of people who have been led to believe that I am there to teach them. Sometimes I am open to the Spirit's movement in these uncomfortable moments, and then I learn something new. At other times I insist upon appearing in charge, and, as a result, learn nothing. I am grateful for those occasions when the classroom has become a learning environment for us all. Some of what appears in these pages is the result of those times.

Most of what is written here, however, is based on my thirty-five years as a full-time church musician prior to becoming a professor in an Episcopal seminary. This book attempts to address clergy of various denominations, but, in the interest of full disclosure, I speak as an Episcopalian—the only way I can. Though raised a Baptist (and ordained in that tradition), I have also worked for Lutherans, Methodists, Presbyterians, and Roman Catholics. (For five years I also sang for High Holy Days in the choir of a Reform Jewish Temple, a rich experience that instructed me in the roots of Christian liturgy.) Most of my time as a church musician, however, has been spent in Episcopal parishes. During my years as a church musician, I worked under the supervision of some thirteen clergy. These priests and pastors showed a wide range of theological perspectives, from the conservative and evangelical to the liberal and social activist. They also subscribed to a wide variety of liturgical practices, from the highly ritualized Anglo-Catholic to the spontaneous charismatic. When I was willing to learn, each of them taught me something, for which I am grateful. I hope these pages reflect something of their patient guidance as well as the work of that consummate teacher, the Holy Spirit.

WBR
Alexandria, Virginia

CHAPTER ONE

Music Belongs to Everyone

Over my head I hear music in the air,
Over my head I hear music in the air,
Over my head I hear music in the air;
There must be a God somewhere.

The Capacity for Making Music

For many clergy, music elicits fear. How I wish I could take the strangeness out of music for clergy who are afraid of it. Some clergy I've worked with find music to be foreign, mystifying, almost like an occult art that only belongs to a select few. I hope to demonstrate that even though there are people with extraordinary talent, and even though some clergy don't comprehend its written language, music is available to everyone.

Most cultures on earth love music. Music making seems to be one of the activities that characterizes us as human. Though musical style varies greatly from one group to another, as well as from one era to another, music seems omnipresent. Humans are a music-making species.

God has greatly gifted us with this amazing dimension of life, and we are immeasurably enriched because of it. Every great congregation has music as a vital component, often widely diverse, but essential.

Why, then, for many in the human family, including clergy, is music confounding, bewildering, puzzling, mysterious, and a language they don't understand? Such persons are daunted by those who appear to understand music, who display a richer appreciation than they, and who also seem to have a special insight into what makes music work. Sometimes the fear arises from unfamiliarity with the written symbols of music. But reading music and enjoying music are not necessarily related. I will argue below that (1) the language of music can be learned like any other language, and (2) a person may also experience great joy from music without knowing the written language.

Are there those whose very birthright places them among the cognoscenti—those who know—while others simply must remain forever unenlightened? Are a few people on earth blessed with a special sense that the remainder of humanity must live without—people who hear, who understand, who perceive music with utter ease?

Art educator Betty Edwards, who wrote the book *Drawing on the Right Side of the Brain*,[5] teaches people to observe objects in a different way so that they can begin to draw. She recalls that even as a child, she saw things in a manner that allowed her to reproduce them graphically. The ability to see shapes and forms readily transferable to paper or canvas was always easy for her.

In the same way, hearing, responding to, and reproducing musical sounds is easier for some people than for others. Oliver Sachs, a noted neurologist and popular author who is also a musician, wrote a fascinating book called *Musicophilia*[6] in which he documents case studies of people who have an extraordinary ability to hear music, as well as the opposite—those whose ability is impaired. He recounts absorbing stories of people with unusual, sometimes even curious, musical ability. For example, one out of every two thousand people displays a phenomenon called "synesthesia." Such persons relate specific musical sounds to corresponding colors. While for most of us this is true at the level of metaphor ("that brilliant chord is fire-engine red"), for synesthetes, the correspondence is not metaphorical at all, but literal and consistent. Sachs tells of the composer Michael Torke who, when he was five years old, told his piano teacher that he liked that "blue piece." When she asked which piece he meant, he answered, the one in the key of D major. "D major is blue."[7]

Scientists debate among themselves over the origins of musical talent—is it genetic or environmental, nature or nurture?—but most are agreed that some people have a heightened capacity for creating and perceiving music. There are people who seem predisposed to extraordinary musical talent.

The truth is, however, that nearly everyone is blessed with the ability to appreciate, and, indeed, at some level to perform music. In some cultures it is assumed that everyone will be involved in music making. Indeed, in the U.S. this assumption also prevailed in an earlier era of our society. As the availability of recorded music has increased and our own participation in music dwindled, music has become a commodity to be consumed more than a group activity. We are intimidated by the sophisticated, nearly perfect performances in recorded music, which let us judge our own efforts unworthy. Whereas manual laborers used to sing songs to alleviate the boredom of repetitive work, today their successors are more likely to listen to recorded music.

Just look at the definition of the "music store." What a music store is has changed radically in the last half-century, signaling a dramatic shift in attitude. When I was a boy, a music store was a place that sold instruments and sheet music, which suggested that you bought things there that help you make music. Those stores sometimes also had departments that sold phonograph recordings, but their primary merchandise was instruments. Now shift to today. When we see a sign at the mall saying "music store," what is sold inside? Probably compact discs, no instruments at all, much less sheet music. While I don't suggest that this change is ipso facto a bad thing, it does represent a quantum leap in our culture. What it says to me is this: We are more likely to be consumers of music than producers. Indeed, church is one of the few remaining environments in U.S. culture where people are expected to make music.

For whatever reason, it has become fashionable in our society to make extravagant claims of one's lack of musical ability. Teachers of music grow weary of those who groan comments like, "You have never heard anybody as bad as I am." Despite these insecurities, most people have the capacity to appreciate and perform music to some degree. A person's exposure to music, especially at an early age, may play an important role in the ability to enjoy music, but in truth almost no one is devoid of musicality. With few exceptions—and these are nearly always due to rare genetic conditions, disease, or accidents—all people are able to appreciate music.

The Language of Music

There is, however, a distinction between appreciating music and knowing the language of music. Just like French, Zulu, or Tagalog, music has vocabulary, syntax, and grammar. Learning the language of music is no more difficult than learning any of these verbal languages. In fact, it is easier, because, in most instances, new students of music have been listening to a musical language all their lives. While the study of Zulu for a nonnative necessitates listening to words that sound strange, the sounds of music have already been in the ear for the duration of one's life. Learning the rudiments of music is simply a matter of connecting symbols and procedures to sounds that are already familiar. Becoming conversant with the language of music is an ordinary and easily achievable goal.[8]

The phrase "music is the international language" is inaccurate and misleading. While a French person might derive a great deal of pleasure in listening to the music of the German composer J. S. Bach, this is because the musics of France and Germany have a common ancestry, the result being that the languages are not too dissimilar from each other. If the same French person were to listen to a piece of classical music from India, or to music that is native to an isolated tribe in South America, that person would likely perceive the music to be confusing, if not downright cacophony. Musical languages vary greatly around the globe, as well as from one era to another.

This story will illustrate. Wycliffe missionary linguists travel to remote parts of the world to translate the Bible into local languages, a project that usually takes ten years or more.[9] This long and arduous process gives the linguists time to come to a deep understanding of the local culture.

In correspondence with a Wycliffe missionary linguist, I learned about the Canela people, who live in a remote, isolated part of Brazil in the Amazon rain forest.[10] Jack and Jo Popjes, the Canadian missionary linguists who went to live with the Canelas, were fascinated with their music, which sounded like nothing they had ever heard. Even though the missionaries were musically trained, they couldn't make sense of the Canelas' music, even after twenty years of effort. Having heard Canela music for myself, I can attest that it is the most exotic music I have ever experienced. Let me describe just one feature of it. Canela music cannot be played on a piano, because there are extra notes that would fall "in the cracks" between the keys of a conventional piano. That is to say, Canela music has more possible pitches than conventional Western music.[11]

For the Canadians, trying to sing along with these indigenous people, even after years of exposure to their music, proved only frustrating. They were eager for the Canelas to compose new songs, so that their worship music would be indigenous, arising from their own culture and experience. Unfortunately the Canelas had no concept of composing new music, because from their perspective the music that formed their repertoire had simply always existed. The missionaries, therefore, had to look elsewhere if there was to be Canela-style Christian hymnody. Contacting a friend who specialized in analyzing the music of indigenous people, the Popjeses were able to create some twenty hymns, Canela-style, mostly with scriptural texts.[12]

The moment of reckoning came when the linguists demonstrated the songs to the Canelas. "It was like throwing gasoline on a campfire!"[13] Upon hearing the songs, the Canelas reacted with great excitement, imploring the linguists to teach them the new music. They wanted to know what tribe had taught the North Americans the songs, because they couldn't imagine that foreigners had made them up. The linguists wept with joy. One Canela man, with tears in his eyes, exulted, "You gave us the book in which God speaks to us, but your friend Tom gave us songs in which we speak to God."[14]

Before the concept existed in missions that indigenous peoples should have their own Christian music, missionaries taught native peoples Western hymnody. Despite the fact that it sometimes made no sense to the people, the practice persisted. Even today, Christians in parts of Africa, for example, sing late nineteenth-century American white gospel hymns, because these were popular in the missionaries' homeland when they arrived in Africa. One of the problems with songs of faith belonging to another culture is that this inscribes Christianity as a foreign religion.

Had the Wycliffe people insisted upon teaching the Canelas "Amazing grace," "Come, thou fount," or Bach chorales, as lovely as those are, they wouldn't have gotten very far. Just as the missionaries' English was foreign to the Canelas, so was their musical language. They had labored hard to speak the Canela's verbal language, and an equal amount of work was required for them to learn the musical language.

There is no "right" system of music—none that is more correct than all other musics on earth. Until rather recently, musicology was Eurocentric in orientation. Western European music was assumed to be the standard, and all others were relegated to an inferior status. Westerners seemed to believe that given enough time, all other cultures would eventually catch up. This Eurocentricity is seen to some extent in the label "ethnic music," meaning the music of cultures outside Western Europe (and, by extension, the U.S. and other predominantly Anglo cultures). This terminology carries the implicit assumption that European music is the norm, placing all others outside the norm.

Careful research by musicologists has demonstrated that music from certain other cultures is far more intricate than European music in specific respects. Music from India, for example, is more melodically complex than European music. Indian *ragas*, intricate melodic formulae, are extremely sophisticated, requiring extensive study.

Likewise, African music is more rhythmically complex than European music. Western missionaries, upon first encountering African music, are said to have declared it unrhythmic, incredible as that sounds. Apparently African percussion music was so vastly complex that it surpassed the missionaries' comprehension, so they judged it arbitrary and disorganized. Now, of course, musicians recognize that the music of sub-Saharan Africa is highly developed rhythmically, and not easily understood by Westerners.

Even within the same culture, two people may have widely divergent responses to music. When I was in seminary, a neighbor of mine asked me to listen to a recording of his favorite piece of music. I agreed, asking him if I could also share a favorite of mine with him, to which he consented. First he played a piece of country music, which I determined to listen to as carefully as possible.

The truth is that even though it was not my cup of tea, I was glad to hear something that meant a lot to him. My seminary colleague was surprised that I was such a stranger to his music, and he was incredulous that I had never heard of the artist.

Next it was my turn, and I played what at the time was my favorite composition, an English cathedral anthem by Benjamin Britten, *Festival te Deum.* It met with a rather amused response: "Well, Roberts, that's just fine if that's what you want to listen to." He didn't seem to mind Britten's music; it just didn't have any effect on him.

Neither his music nor mine was "right"; they just used different languages. He was moved by one, I by the other. I would never suggest that this neighbor was "wrong" in his musical taste, but rather that he is free to like what he chooses, and I hope he would accord me the same liberty. In fact, differing preferences in music might be seen as an extension of the discussion of spiritual gifts in 1 Corinthians 12. It takes all of us, with our orientation to different music, to make up the complete Body of Christ.

There is a close connection between cultural identity and specific musical styles. While there are different languages of music, within those languages there are regional "dialects" and "accents." Despite the fact that my seminary friend and I had grown up in neighboring states, we responded differently to the two examples because of our respective musical languages—both derived from Western European tradition (though his might also have contained blues, and, therefore, African elements).

Often, in describing their inability to perceive music as well as they'd like, people say they don't "understand" music. Yet understanding is probably less important than exposure. A professor of mine said that the old cliché "I don't know much about music, but I know what I like" should really be "I don't know much about music, but I *like* what I *know*."[15]

Most people enjoy their favorite music, whether it is classical European or Argentine dance music, without knowing much about its structure or theoretical components. This lack of technical knowledge does not prevent someone from being deeply moved by the music. Its impact comes from years of exposure to music, stored in the mind and heart, and the associated experiences and feelings. Old familiar sounds, or new sounds related to the old ones, evoke an emotional response as they fall on our ears and trigger our memory.

When one has had a profound spiritual experience, hearing the music later that was connected with it powerfully recalls the event or even evokes new spiritual response.

Predictably, the kind of music that a person is exposed to before adulthood is likely to elicit lifelong responses. Certainly new types of music, as well as further examples of familiar styles, may be added throughout life, just as we may develop new tastes in food as we age. There may always be, however, a particular fondness for the music of one's youth, just as there is for the food of one's home.

A friend of mine who loved working with children's choirs said, "I figure that one of the most important things I do is to sock away snippets of Mozart into their little temporal lobes, so that they will love it for their lifetime."

Still, it is never too late to learn to love new music, and we may find that repeated exposure to music even later in life elicits strong feelings about it. Hearing a little music a lot has a greater impact than hearing a lot of music a little. Repetition of a composition allows it really to belong to you.

For clergy, an ability to learn and respond to new music is vitally important. As they move to different congregations, clergy will encounter a new repertoire, new "old favorites," dearly loved by that group of people. Sensitive pastors will enlarge their own repertoires to encompass the music of their new congregations.

Entering the World of Music

Clergy who have felt marginalized from the experience of music may be encouraged to know that everybody can grow in their appreciation of music, and that everybody can contribute as members of a musical spiritual community. It is most unfortunate that some clergy have been told that they don't have the musical skills to participate. A thoughtless (and, moreover, misinformed) music teacher in their elementary school, or even, God forbid, a church musician, may have convinced them that they couldn't sing, and urged them to be quiet. It is an act of unimaginable cruelty to take the gift of song away from a person. Surely such a gift is the birthright of every human being, and in the service of worship it is irreplaceable.

While not every person may be able to sing as an accomplished vocalist possessing natural talent and extensive training, these are not the only singers invited to the banquet, thanks be to God. When it comes to congregational singing, *participation* is more important than *quality*. Though it is possible (and desirable) for congregations to improve their singing, the primary goal of congregational song is opening one's heart and voice to God. In that process we experience the transforming, empowering sense of corporate worship.

Clergy who have felt excluded from music need to know that they are fully welcome participants. Surely God's own invitation trumps anyone else's careless act of exclusion. Often private sessions with a sensitive pastoral musician, or worship in small groups, perhaps with other clergy, will provide opportunities to recover one's confidence as a singing worshipper.

Music is God's gift to all humanity, not to a select few. Clergy who fully participate in worship not only sing health into their own souls, but also model for those whom they lead that a vital church includes a singing congregation.

CHAPTER TWO

Moving from Musician as Performer to Musician as Pastor

Lord, Oh, hear me prayin', Lord, Oh, hear me prayin',
Oh, hear me prayin'
I want to be more holy ev'ry day.
Like Peter when you said to him, Feed my sheep,
Like Peter when you said to him, Feed my sheep,
Like Peter when you said to him, Feed my lambs,
Like Peter when you said to him, Feed my lambs.

"Leaders in church in whatever area are *Pastors, Teachers* and *Performers* in exactly that order."[1] Alec Wyton (1921–2007), who was a well-known English-American church musician and teacher, created this truism. Implicit in his statement is a philosophy of church music.

Clergy need a basic philosophy of church music for several reasons. First, when hiring someone—be it a part-time musician for a few hours a week in a small parish, or a full-time person for a large church or cathedral—the pastor or priest needs some basis for a conversation. What tenets do we agree upon? Where do we differ? Has this applicant given any consideration to what he or she thinks about the practice of church music? Especially in the case of the part-time musician who has another primary vocation, she or he may have given little thought to what makes church music effective. The clergy may feel that other qualities warrant hiring this candidate anyway (or maybe no one else is available!). As we will discuss elsewhere, the wise clergy will then begin training the part-time person to develop an understanding of church music.

Perhaps the following brief discussion will guide clergy in thinking about a philosophy of church music. For those seeking a deeper study, there are more comprehensive materials.[2]

Alec Wyton's formula—Pastor, Teacher, Performer, in that order—is a good basis for a philosophy of church music. When I ask future clergy if they see this statement as controversial, most of them answer no. If this is true, it shows how accepted this attitude has become, at least among ordained ministers. When Wyton first wrote these words, his formula understandably sparked a debate— at least in the denomination he served.[3] Even today it often provokes lively discussion. Why so?

In our standard stereotype, the traditional role of the church musician still looks like this: He or she is engaged to direct the choirs, perhaps also to play the organ. The musician prepares music for worship, seeing to it that the music fits the liturgy. Those employing the church musician hope that the music will bring beauty and enrichment to worship and offend as few people as possible. On the face of it, there's nothing wrong with this picture. In many ways it reflects the position of my own denomination several decades ago when I first began the practice of church music.

I compare this view of the church musician to the worker you hire to paint the church steeple. You don't care how he feels about steeples, or even what he thinks about the churches underneath them. You just want to know if he can paint the steeple. Applied to the parish organist or choir director, this would be what I call the "steeple-painter church musician." How such persons feel about faith or ministry simply isn't germane, as long as they don't interfere with the larger work of the church. And perhaps for some parishes this model still works just fine. It is to the clergy of the other parishes, however, that I'm speaking—those clergy expect that a church musician will be a partner in ministry.

Pastor

In addition to the typical musical responsibilities, church musicians will lead those in their charge in such a way that cares for their spirits as well as for their voices. It will be entirely appropriate, for example, for rehearsals to include prayer at the beginning or ending. In two of my former parishes, the service of Compline (the final service of the day in religious communities) was part of our denomination's tradition, and so we sang this brief service at the conclusion of each rehearsal. There was a time during Compline for choir members to pray their own thanksgivings or petitions aloud or silently.

A number of years ago, when I had just begun work in a new parish, a long-standing member of the choir's bass section approached me with the blustery admonition, "You know, we don't come here to pray. We come to sing." He clearly expected the steeple-painter church musician, and I did not meet his expectations.

Leaders of any group will encounter many people who still expect the predecessor's practices. When moving, a new leader naturally wants to take charge but may wonder whether to fulfill people's expectations or to teach them new ones. In reality, a combination of the two is essential to enlightened and successful leadership.

Because I am a slow learner, we continued to pray in these choir rehearsals, and in the case of the blustery bass, praying together was something that he either adapted to, or else learned to put up with. Eventually members of this choir became a spiritual community to

21

each other, something that nearly always happens after people begin to pray together. When someone in the choir was sick or going through a crisis, it became entirely natural after a time for others in the group to extend a caring hand. Sometimes I the leader didn't even know when such acts of charity occurred. They simply became natural among the choir. Another joyful outcome of this increased intimacy was extraordinary parties. People who come to love each other not only care for one another, but they also enjoy being together.

Pastoring in Time of Crisis

A choir member approached me at a time when he was questioning deep aspects of his sexual identity. I deferred to a trained professional, sensing his need for therapy. Eventually he created major changes in his life, which resulted in a happier, better-integrated life for himself and his family.

Parishioners active in music, when there is something in their lives that needs attention, will often seek out the church musician even before the priest or pastor. Participants in the music ministry may feel safer initially in sharing sensitive matters with the church musician than with the clergy. This is not a negative comment on the clergyperson, but reflects the large amounts of time in rehearsals and services the parishioner has spent with the musician. Naturally more time together may build trust, allowing the person to experience fruitful healing. Church musicians who understand their pastoral role will exercise great care, however, to refer parishioners, when appropriate, to the clergy or to a professional counselor. Those parish musicians with a healthy sense of self will be grateful that someone in need has sought them out, but won't allow this to lure them into difficult counseling issues that require particular training.

The church musician as Pastor will also find it appropriate to visit choir members who are confined to home or hospital. As all ministers (lay or ordained) discover, these are times when people are most vulnerable and conscious of their deepest longings. These are the moments when they are likely to dig their roots into their spiritual community. No minister will want to miss an opportunity to engage with people in their greatest time of need. These are surely some of the most rewarding opportunities of ministry. When clergy and musicians cultivate healthy relations with each other (see chapter three), there will be no competition or conflict in pastoring, but a spirit of cooperation and trust.

A colleague tells the story of a hospitalized choir member whom he, the new church musician, went to visit. It had not been the custom at this parish for the organist-choirmaster to call on people in the hospital, and so the patient was utterly surprised by his visit. Not only did this move serve to bond the relationship between choir member and parish, it also began a decades-long friendship between singer and church musician that was a delight to both.

Another place for clergy to encourage musicians to employ their pastoral skills is in choir rehearsals. In these settings church musicians who are sensitive to the movement of the Spirit will find a moment to reflect upon a particularly insightful text. Choristers who sing in choirs year after year inevitably absorb the magnificent language of great religious poetry and Scripture. Sometimes the director's simplest comment will call their attention to a phrase they might otherwise have missed, which will be meaningful to them for years to come. Long-winded instructional soliloquies are not as effective as short, well-placed remarks. Clergy are sometimes surprised when people, years after the fact, remark on a comment made in a sermon. Likewise, people astonish church musicians by repeating theological reflections that were made years earlier.

Often, the most profound comments are made by the singers themselves, and this is nowhere more dramatic than when spoken by children. As an illustration, here are two contrasting occasions that happened within weeks of each other. Both were choir rehearsals in which we were practicing an anthem[4] on the passionate text of George Herbert's "Love bade me welcome" (see page 124).[5] The first of these rehearsals was with an adult choir in the Southwest U.S. One of the tenors said, "I haven't got the faintest idea what this text is about. Could you explain it?" It was a text I had lived with for many years, and it was easy to take two minutes to tell what I thought it meant.

Three weeks later found me at a rehearsal of a regional festival of boy choirs in western New York. Having had the recent experience of the adult singer who was confused by the Herbert text, I thought it might be valuable to take a moment to discuss it with the boys. Fortunately I decided to ask them first if they had any notion what the poem was saying. A third-grader named Matt spoke up. How I wish I could quote him verbatim, but the gist of what he said was: "God invites this person to come in, and the person says, 'I'm not good enough,' and God says, 'That's okay. I've made you good enough.' And then the person comes in and sits down and eats." It was simple, eloquent, and profound. Blinking back a few tears, I said to him, "Matt, not only do I have nothing to add, but also I think if the priest doesn't have a sermon prepared for this afternoon's service, you should stand up in the pulpit and repeat what you've just said." The boys laughed, but they also understood that their colleague had spoken wisely.

Here a third-grader had done the teaching, undoubtedly making a far greater impression on the other boys in the choir than if I had explained the poem. The eighteenth-century English poet William Cowper could have easily had Matt in mind when he penned, "Sometimes a light surprises the Christian while he sings."[6]

Of Alec Wyton's three roles for the church musician—Pastor, Teacher, Performer—Pastor may be the most uneasy for musicians. This is because many church musicians are trained in secular conservatories or state schools, where pastoral issues are not likely to have been addressed. The role of Performer is made centrally clear, as is Teacher, but that of Pastor may not be mentioned. It may become the clergy-supervisors' task to help church musicians to understand this aspect of their role. Because in most instances clergy education is so different from music education, clergy will often find themselves functioning as church music educators— that is, they will need to encourage musicians to grow into church musicians.

Teacher

How do clergy help musicians understand this function? The illustration above, where the theology of George Herbert's poem was discussed in two choir rehearsals, flows easily to a discussion of the church musician's role as Teacher. A discussion of the anthem text may spiritually nurture choir members, but it also enriches them educationally. Because many modern schools give scant attention to the study of poetry, reflecting on the structure and content of sung texts helps open new worlds to singers.

The role of Teacher will be very clear to church musicians with extensive training in conducting, because a conductor is, by nature, a teacher. He or she is accustomed to giving correction in the course of rehearsals. The proficient conductor, however, will have not only a "corrective approach" to rehearsals, but also a "directive approach"; that is to say, the conductor will not only correct mistakes—notes, pronunciation, tone production, blend, etc.—but will also have a "silent curriculum," a series of major goals for the singers or instrumentalists to accomplish. Such goals may include improvement of music reading, techniques for communicating the texts more clearly, and learning to blend one's voice (or instrument) with others. People feel good about themselves when they sense that they are being challenged and stimulated, and when this leads to improving their skills. The church musician as Teacher can foster such growth.

Many choir singers spend decades in a church choir. During their long experience there is no reason for not making huge gains in their abilities. In a recent parish I served, choir members began the evening with a short class on music reading and vocal skills, followed by a buffet supper, then rehearsal. As choir singers' skills increased, so did their level of confidence and their sense of fulfillment as leaders of worship.

Clergy may encourage church musicians to extend their role as Teacher, however, far beyond the choral or instrumental rehearsal room. The staff and the congregation may also benefit from this teaching role. If the part-time musician is able to attend staff meetings, both musician and staff will benefit. As the parish staff gathers to plan worship, the pastor or priest may invite the musician to demonstrate new materials, or teach a new piece of music that will later be sung by the congregation. Incorporating music into a staff meeting can add a light touch to what sometimes becomes intense discussion. Why not ask the church musician to teach staff members new music as part of their staff worship together?

In a larger sense, the church musician is really in the role of Teacher with the congregation, true whether the musician is full-time or part-time. Many parishes create an opportunity for the church musician to introduce a new piece of music just prior to the worship service. As a cautionary note, some churches maintain the custom of congregational members' entering the church in silence and praying until the service begins; in this case, a preservice rehearsal needs to be handled carefully, allowing time for silent praying before the liturgy starts. When possible, such a rehearsal helps parishioners to participate confidently in the new piece of music during the service.

Some congregations enjoy having hymn sings. These may take place in conjunction with a service, or, an altogether different idea, as part of a social event, such as a parish dinner or holiday party. Wise clergy urge the musician to use music as a way to foster camaraderie and bonhomie. Besides the enjoyment they afford, these are opportunities for teaching and encouraging congregational singers. The church musician as Teacher who handles these occasions with humor and a light touch will be most successful.

Still other opportunities exist for clergy to encourage the musician as Teacher. The church musician may be asked to write articles for the parish newsletter or website, or to present forums on topics of worship and musical interest to the congregation. In a recent parish I served, a member of the congregation expressed a strong interest in learning more about the music the choir was singing in an upcoming festival, and suggested that a forum be scheduled the week before this event. The rector agreed. This resulted in a series that continued throughout the remainder of my tenure in that parish. Many parishioners enjoyed learning about the new, often challenging music, benefiting from the program suggested by a congregation member.

Most people enjoy the action of learning something new. When clergy involve the church musician in the role of Teacher, it not only gratifies peoples' need to learn, it also offers new opportunities for him or her to engage with the congregation.

Performer

No aspect of the church musician's identity is likely to create more controversy than the role of Performer. In my seminary classes, future clergy are often very disturbed even by the very use of the word. Musicians, who in many cases have been seriously studying their art since the age of six or seven, understand the performance dimension of their work. From the beginning of music study as children, they are called upon to perform as a way of demonstrating what they have learned, and as practice in connecting with an audience. Musicians are always pretty clear about their role as Performer.

For many clergy, the word "perform" is a great stumbling block. I have witnessed heated discussions about performance many times. Much difficulty stems from the negative connotations of the word, which I address below. Performance touches on any church leader—that is, anyone who stands out from the congregation, not just musicians. Preachers are performers just as surely as musicians are. In fact, it might be said that preachers who don't understand the performance aspect of their art will probably never be very good at it. There are performance skills to be learned in both music and homiletics, and as with many tasks, the most successful performer is the one whose skill is invisible and unselfconscious.

What upsets us, then, about this word "performer?" Doubtless it is the unsettling awareness of the role of one's ego in performance. Few people enjoy a performance that merely glorifies the performer, not just in church. In a fine performance of a Shakespearean play, the audience expects to focus on the wonderful words of the Bard, to connect with the characters, to be caught up in the plot. As we watch the play, we want to be more conscious of the story than we are of the performers per se. It makes us uncomfortable if the performers call attention to themselves as actors. The same is true in church, whether for preachers, musicians, or liturgical leaders. Those who effectively "perform" their role do so with such a combination of skill and integrity that worshippers do not focus upon the leader, but are drawn into a transforming relationship with God.

Sometimes we mistakenly judge another person's motives, a dangerous pursuit. When this happens it likely means that we are projecting onto another person our own suspicions about the role of ego. I can recall more than one such scenario. After a service someone comes up to the pastor and says, "That singer seemed to be really full of herself when she was up there singing today." Knowing her far better than the person speaking, the pastor is forced to respond, "No, actually there is hardly anyone I know who is more centered on worship when she is singing." At such a moment I take comfort in 1 Samuel 16:7. "People look on the outward appearance, but God looks on the heart."

Still, it is good for us to remind ourselves of just what our role is in worship. Like a good Shakespearean, we want people to focus not on the performer, but on the character (the God of our salvation) and on the story (the drama of the liturgy).

Pastor, Teacher, Performer

Nobody is born a pastor. The role is acquired through life experiences, education, and prayer. Clergy may find themselves working with a musician, part-time or full-time, for whom incorporating the role of pastor into music ministry is a strange notion. Keeping the larger picture in mind, however, transformation is the very nature of the church's enterprise—transformation not only among the church's members, but also within its leadership.

CHAPTER THREE

Clergy–Musician Relationships

Can't you live humble?
Praise King Jesus!
Can't you live humble
To the dyin' Lamb?
Lightnin' flashes, thunders roll,
Make me think of my poor soul.
Come here, Jesus, come here please,
See me, Jesus, on my knees.

The Problem

The state of clergy-musician relationships in today's churches is often abysmally bad, making us want to echo Rodney King's plaintive question after the horrendous L.A. uprising of 1992, "Can't we all just get along?" A few clergy may feel that the power differential forces the musician to do all the work in maintaining harmonious relations. "After all, I am the boss, so they'll just have to figure out how to work with me." Most clergy, however, have enough sense of justice to want to do what is necessary to build and sustain pleasant and effective working relationships with their staff. Parishioners certainly notice. And when church leaders model healthy relationships, congregations are likely to mirror this behavior, causing their work to flourish both inside and outside the parish.

The work I do often takes me to meetings where clergy predominate. I also attend meetings where church musicians are the majority. Just let the subject of musicians arise in a clergy group, or the topic of clergy in a musicians group, and the sparks begin to fly. Given enough time, the conversation sometimes degenerates into war stories. "If you think that's something, listen to this!"

The comments from clergy often sound like this: "I wish I could figure out how to work with this temperamental, opinionated musician." "We'd like to broaden our congregation's music repertoire, but our musician is a staunch traditionalist and will not hear of it." "Our musician doesn't really seem to care too much for church. I get the feeling she puts up with it just so she can do her music." "The other members of the staff complain about how much money we spend on music, compared with their own areas of ministry." "There are some changes I've been wanting to make, but the musician is deeply entrenched with her strong following, and I don't dare do anything to offend the music crowd." "The musician in our parish has no training in liturgy, but that doesn't keep him from thinking he knows everything." "No matter what I suggest to our musician, her nose gets out of joint." "We're paying our musician about the same as other parishes in the area, but he constantly tells me he's underpaid."

Musicians' comments about clergy are equally charged. "I don't think my clergy's seminary taught him the first thing about worship. If they did, it certainly doesn't show." "My clergy are always after me to do what I call 'camp music,' and, in my book, it's all trash. I just flatly refuse, and the choirs support me." "My pastor (or priest) didn't grow up in this tradition, and she always wants to do this music from her background, which has nothing to do with our church." "The clergy here don't care about liturgy. All they care about is their own preaching." "My clergyperson is always telling me what music to do. He has no music training at all and asks for the most ridiculous things. I'm the expert. Why doesn't he just leave it up to me?" "How can our church pride itself on its equal-justice stance when my salary is about half the senior minister's?"

At a meeting some years ago, a participant mentioned an electronic gadget that "accompanies" congregational hymn singing. A bishop who was present said with a smile, "Good! Bring it on. Then I won't have to deal with these touchy musicians." A church musician piped up, "And considering how bad most preaching is, let's just listen to recordings of great sermons on Sunday morning." "Touché," said the bishop, and laughter saved the day.

Sometimes, however, it's no laughing matter. Relationships get broken, careers destroyed, parishioners divided into camps, lives damaged, wounds nursed for years. If this is unfamiliar to you, good; it means that, so far, life has spared you this blow. In fact, I am a church musician who has had the joy of many healthy and happy relationships with supervising clergy. Nevertheless, this can be a widespread problem that will not go away by avoidance. What on earth causes such anger and resentment between people who must work together and are otherwise skilled at human interaction?

Clergy and Musicians as Performers

When I discuss clergy-musician relationships with seminarians, I begin with the following question: "Do you know what the plural of prima donna is?" After an appropriate silence, I answer my own question: "There isn't one."

In the sense that both the clergyperson and church musician are performers, they occupy the same "stage." Unlike opera or theater, in church there's no stage director, no objective person to observe and plot the most effective staging of the drama, no one

33

to sort out who is doing what and how long it takes. In fact, it is usually the senior clergyperson who acts as "director," and she or he is far from objective.

Of course, the ultimate solution to competition for the role of prima donna is that nobody be one. When I accept my role in worship as that of servant, most of the tension can be released. The church prima donna is of no earthly (or heavenly) use. Those parishioners who treat us as celebrities do us no favors, but rather encourage the worst in us. Our work is severely compromised when we bask in our spotlights. Humility is not easy to acquire, and assuming that you have achieved it is an absolute guarantee that you haven't. Someone once quipped, "I certainly am humble, *wasn't* I?"

Even those who knew the earthly Jesus, the perfect example of humility, didn't get it. Take the story of James and John's mother, petitioning Jesus to let her sons sit at Jesus' right and left in the Reign of God. Jesus' teaching on humility—"the last shall be first" (Matt 20:16); "the greatest among you shall be your servant" (Matt 23:11)—has never been very popular anywhere, church included. In those rare cases when servant leadership is taken seriously, however, the power of God's Spirit is truly unleashed.

Wise clergy seek out trusted persons to fill the missing role of "stage director." Clergy will want to ask questions of such a confidant, "How is the worship service working? Never mind my ego needs. Please give me the unvarnished truth. How am I doing? How about the other 'players' in the 'drama'? What can we do to improve? How can we make the worship better? What do we need to do to get ourselves out of the way so that God can be honored?" Out of our human insecurity, we often seek feedback only from those who are uncritically devoted to us. Yet someone who is wise and insightful, who has no ax to grind, no direct stake in the way our particular worship is conducted, and who has the courage to be honest, is worth his or her weight in gold. Robert

Burns' oft-quoted line has it "O wad some Power the giftie gie us/ To see oursels as ithers see us!"[1]

We leaders may even learn something on our own by just sitting out and observing on occasion. Every clergyperson or musician I have ever known who has taken a Sunday off to sit and participate as a member of the congregation comes away with the same report. "I can't believe what I learned!" It is a costly investment, but one with high-yield dividends.

Sharing a small "stage" Sunday after Sunday is not easy. By our very nature we humans are creatures who define our turf. Defending our territory is bred in the bone. Of course, there are many aspects of human behavior that we subject to the Gospel's tempering, and this clearly needs to be one of them. Planning and executing worship together may be difficult, but when leaders approach worship with prayerful humility, and in a spirit of charity, cooperation, and love, the way is smoother, "for love covers a multitude of sins" (1 Peter 4:8).

Differences in Educational Background

Clergy and musicians are each educated differently. They learn conflicting models for their respective work. This is because, for the most part, they train in radically different environments. At an ecumenical gathering of clergy and musicians, participants from a wide range of backgrounds concluded that working relations between priests or pastors and church musicians would be markedly better if we were trained in the same environment.

A few denominations are faithful in this enterprise. Southern Baptists and United Methodists, for example, for many years have had schools of sacred music at their seminaries—departments or schools that train church musicians alongside and with clergy candidates. The National Association of Schools of Music, the major music accrediting organization for academic institutions, lists only three seminary members: the Baptist seminaries in Louisville, New Orleans, and Ft. Worth.

Seminary music schools, in addition to the studio and class work required at any school of music, offer courses in theology, Bible, pastoral care, and Christian education. Since the country's leading School of Sacred Music at Union Seminary (1928–1973) closed, its disappearance has been much lamented. This school produced a number of prominent leaders in church music. Some of its faculty and resources moved to the Yale Institute of Sacred Music (begun in 1972), which has also developed impressive leaders. Its students take advantage of the rich resources at the Yale School of Music and the Yale Divinity School.

Some state universities offer degrees in church music (e.g., Indiana University). Several denominations have colleges that train church musicians, but the institutions charged with preparing leaders in the church—seminaries—for the most part have felt no obligation to train leaders of music. Recently I said to the faculty of the seminary where I teach that the Episcopal Church embodies the Tennessee Williams school of church music education: We have ". . . always depended upon the kindness of strangers."[2] That is, we expect others to train our musicians for us. When they do, we can hardly complain that musicians have been given different values and standards than clergy.

Most denominations are intentional and energetic in training their clergy. They expect that if clergy are to receive the tradition of the church and spend a lifetime leading parishes, they need to be properly prepared. Denominations set aside financial resources, bring together the best minds, build and equip campuses, and provide oversight by boards of interested leaders. That we don't give the same attention to the training of church musicians is outright negligence.

The seminary experience includes not only academic course work to prepare for ministry, but also includes spiritual formation.

Regular chapel services, interaction with faculty, spiritual direction, supervised fieldwork—all these are integral to the development of Christian leaders. In seminary, denominations expect the faith journey of its future leaders to be shaped. The principles the church holds dear are passed on—worship, mission and outreach, Christian education, pastoral care, the history of the church, preaching, biblical languages, theology. Students become steeped in the ethos of their church. Seminaries attempt to provide whatever is needed for parish ministry, including spiritual values and human service.

Meanwhile, future church musicians, studying in conservatories or universities, receive a very different sort of education. Music students concentrate on the acquisition of skills as performers. Usually that emphasis is upon attaining the highest possible quality in performance, so that if students experience excellence in their individual and ensemble performance, both faculty and students consider they have achieved their goal. Courses in music theory, history, and literature exist primarily to develop excellence in performance. There is absolutely nothing wrong with these criteria; they are, however, designed for the world of professional music, not for the church.

When clergy and musicians trained in these radically different perspectives come into the same arena, they come with markedly different goals and assumptions. Theologian and church musician Paul Westermeyer addresses this issue in his excellent book *Te Deum: The Church and Music* in the hypothetical example of a clergyperson and a musician selecting music, each using completely different criteria. "The musician in this instance makes virtually no theological judgment, and the clergy makes no musical judgment. The musician may then accuse the pastor of having no musical understanding, and the pastor is likely to say the musician does not know anything about worship, ethics, people, or evangelism"[3] Comparing the training environments of musician and pastor, it's easy to see why there is such disagreement.

In the Absence of Seminary Music Degrees

Various groups have attempted to fill the void. The College of Church Musicians, headed by eminent musician Leo Sowerby, was a short-lived effort to train church musicians at the Washington National Cathedral from 1962 to 1968. Currently the Leadership Program for Musicians (www.lpm-online.org) is an ecumenical program that trains church musicians in a program of study leading to the LPM Certificate in Church Music. Its comprehensive curriculum is a model that seminaries might well use. The Mentoring Task Force of the Association of Anglican Musicians (www.anglicanmusicians.org) pairs new church musicians with seasoned ones. In addition, some large parishes offer organ scholars or apprentice church musicians the incomparable opportunity of working for a year or two with a master church musician. At the time of this writing, Christ Church in Alexandria, Virginia, is in the process of setting up a fellowship program for emerging church musicians. Upon completing their formal education, fellows will work alongside seasoned clergy and musicians in parishes of several denominations in the Washington, D.C., area, giving them hands-on, practical experience.

Summer music conferences and workshops presently are offered that can help musicians gain skills in church music. Over a period of time, musicians can receive some good training in such informal settings. The Mississippi Conference on Church Music and Liturgy is one example. Church musicians who have attended this conference for a number of years have worked with many leaders in the fields of church music and liturgy. Such summer workshops help church musicians develop confidence in their vocations.

The primary drawback of training at summer conferences and workshops is this: When a church musician gets his training primarily in these settings, it is fragmentary and unsystematic. The musician who attends such sporadic summer study, even at its best, picks up bits of information here and there. Comprehensive, coordinated training in one location would be far preferable.

Seminaries could offer such comprehensive, coordinated training. Even those seminaries that don't offer degree work in music could offer summer courses for church musicians. If seminaries developed a systematic program that was offered over a period of two or three years, church musicians could learn important skills and benefit from the accompanying rich spiritual formation—a program that would have an immediate and far-reaching impact on the church.

Naturally it is a great challenge for the part-time musician to find the time to participate in any of these training schemes. Clergy can encourage their part-time musicians to take advantage of available programs, and can strengthen this support by providing the financial backing necessary. It is amazing to observe how many part-time musicians from tiny parishes attend summer training programs, often at their own expense, and frequently using valuable vacation time from their primary jobs. Clergy and parish backing for such training would not only persuade many more musicians to take advantage of these opportunities, it would also demonstrate justice and fairness toward the profession of church music.

Many times, especially in the case of part-time church musicians, clergy will discover that it is mandatory for them to participate personally in the training of a new musician, especially when the musician has been educated in secular institutions. If the musician has had no exposure to the denomination's tradition, if she wants to develop greater theological insight, or needs to discover access to critical materials and repertoire, the clergy may find themselves, however unintentionally, assuming the role of mentor.

What Can Clergy Do about the Need for Music Leadership?

There are two things that astute clergy can do to promote comprehensive music leadership in the church. First, they can begin by contacting their seminary and pressing them to offer training to church musicians. Whether it be formal curriculum, offered through summer study, or informal workshops, many seminaries already have the resources to make this happen, and training could be put into place in a relatively short time. Better yet, clergy can help provide the funding for their seminaries to start such a program. While clergy usually aren't able to become major donors, they often know parishioners with abundant resources, people who are delighted to support worthy endeavors. If the church cares about music, it will train and equip people to develop rich, effective music ministries.

Second, if the parish employs a part-time musician, clergy can encourage a move toward expanding the position to a full-time one. I have offered clergy this guideline for many years: Hire a full-time musician instead of a third clergyperson. As the parish grows and needs further program leadership, it is wise to add a musician rather than more clergy. A priest friend of mine has implemented this formula in his last two parishes, resulting in remarkable growth. The energy offered by vital church music will more than repay that decision. It is prudent to make sure the salary and benefits are strong enough to attract the best people. Once they have found the best church musician possible, it is good business sense for clergy to build in an annual review of salary and benefits to make sure she is adequately compensated, so that she will stay.

There is an alarming trend in the diminishing number of vocational church musicians, but this trend could be quickly reversed by providing more full-time positions. It is hardly surprising that few young people pursue degrees in organ or church music when the positions are primarily part-time and pay inadequate wages. Without a doubt the supply of qualified church musicians would expand rapidly if attractive employment were made available.

Parishes that are able to move from a part-time music position to a full-time one will notice that outstanding candidates are suddenly at their disposal. When the parish advertises a full-time music position, applications will come from all over the country from musicians whose primary vocational calling is church music. Rather than being limited to the pool of candidates in the immediate area, the parish can cast a wide net and choose from a large list of interested candidates. On rare occasions a parish is blessed to have a wonderful part-time musician who couldn't be better if she were full-time and paid triple her current salary. This, however, is rarely the case. More often the part-time person has another job and limited time for her commitment. A full-time church musician who is (1) musically talented, (2) dynamic and effective as a leader, and (3) spiritually grounded will transform the congregation. The parish itself will grow and flourish.

Moving to Healthy Relationships

What can clergy do to develop good relationships with their musicians? In general, the same principles of any good relationship apply: They spend deliberate time getting to know each other; they don't wait until there is a problem to invest in the relationship; they listen more than they talk; they use "reflective listening" ("Now let me see if I can repeat what you just said."); they show an interest in their colleague's life apart from the workplace; they enjoy the humor of shared situations.

As the employer or supervisor, the clergy can do concrete things to make matters go smoothly. They can:

- make sure there is an up-to-date job description, and that it is *honored* (meaning not adding more and more duties without subtracting others or increasing pay);

- schedule regular evaluations that include a written record of accomplishments and needs for improvement;

- give merit raises that reward good work and outstanding leadership;

- make sure that salary reviews include a comparison of equivalent pay in other institutions, as well as the current cost of living in the area;

- praise, praise, praise, being specific and honest; praise in public, correct in private;

- provide the tools and resources necessary for the music colleague to do good work;

- encourage creativity and initiative;

- include the colleague in decision making that affects her/ his work (like the budget);

- make sure there is adequate time off, especially following the hyperdemanding seasons of Christmas and Easter;

- provide resources, encouragement, and opportunities for continuing education and professional development;

- schedule periodic opportunities to dream together about long-term and intermediate visions;

- develop a timeline that implements goals that are agreed upon.

Besides such commonsense principles that improve any employer/ employee relationship, there are specific ways clergy can encourage the musical and liturgical work of the church musician. They can:

- schedule occasional visits to choir rehearsals, giving a word of thanks, encouragement, and support to the choristers;

- offer to lead a prayer with the singers before worship;

- provide the opportunity in staff meetings for the musician to introduce new music that is coming up in worship;

- make time in staff meetings to discuss philosophies of worship;

- look for ways to integrate the musician into the life of the parish other than worship services (music at parties or parish meals);

- have a private discussion with the musician before proposing dramatic changes that will affect the music program in any way.

There is every reason for relationships between clergy and musicians to be healthy, productive, and enjoyable. Intentionality, clarity, trust, honesty, humor, and, above all, God's good grace will make it so.

CHAPTER FOUR

Classical Music vs. Popular Music: A War over Nothing

Wade in the watuh,
Wade in the watuh, chillen,
Wade in the watuh,
God's a-gonna trouble the watuh.

"What is the greatest challenge you face?" This was among the questions asked in a recent survey of the members of a professional organization of church musicians. Overwhelmingly the answer was "negotiating the diversity of liturgical musical styles."[1] The respondents intended to convey their unease about using music in popular styles and the music of ethnic minorities. Nothing generates such anxiety and controversy among classically trained church musicians as this issue; nothing else raises the level of fear and perplexity. Besides, it can become a bone of contention between clergy and musicians, exacerbating any inherent tensions. What causes this reaction, and what can be done to unite people who are divided over it?

Talking about the subject is so difficult that even the terminology itself can set people on edge. Thankfully the labels for music in the classical tradition like "legit" (short for "legitimate") have dropped from usage. The biggest problem with calling any music "legitimate" is that other types of music, by implication, are automatically "illegitimate." Likewise the term "serious music" is unhelpful, because music in the classical tradition can itself be light, playful, or humorous, while music in the popular tradition can be quite somber. The term "art music" is also useless since it implies a lack of artistry in other types of music. Even the designation "classical" can be misleading. While we use it in a general sense, "classical" is also the standard classification of the specific period in Western European music history, the Viennese Classical Period, when Haydn (1732–1809), Mozart (1756–1791), and Beethoven (1770–1827) were active, producing music that was characterized by a particular form, style, and clarity of expression.

Wiley Hitchcock, a leading scholar of American music, coined the terms "music of the vernacular tradition" and "music of the cultivated tradition."[2] These labels are more useful, differentiating between music in popular styles, "vernacular music" that absorbs elements from the surrounding culture, and music containing ingredients "cultivated" from European composers like Bach, Mozart, and Beethoven. Hitchcock's terms are helpful in that they are descriptive, avoiding value judgments about either type of music; one is not automatically labeled "better" than the other. We absorb vernacular music in much the same way that we acquire our native language; it is all around us, and we come to know it easily. Often (but not always) people who love classical music have had their interest in it cultivated—that is, they have intentionally devoted attention to it (and perhaps had instruction in it).

For the sake of this discussion, we will use the terms "classical music" (in its general sense) and "popular religious song." Carol Doran coined the latter term in her excellent essay of the same name,[3] the background for this present discussion.

Some parishes have an exclusive diet of classical music, while others use only popular religious song. Those who read what follows in order to be affirmed for the exclusive practice of either may be disappointed. On the other hand, if you would like to think further about this controversial subject, this discussion may open some new avenues of thought and possibility.

How Music Comes and Goes in the Church's Repertoire

Doran's essay "Popular Religious Song" employs a very helpful model for understanding how any type of music gains common use, and then either remains in the repertoire or drops out and disappears from use. She adapts an illustration that Dutch theologian Edward Schillebeeckx created to explain cultural shifts.[4]

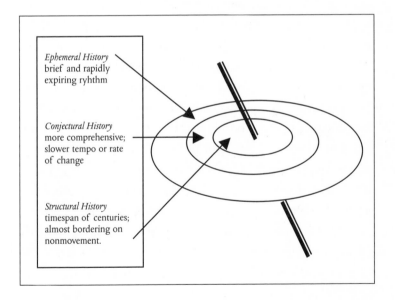

Schillebeeckx's model has three concentric circles on a common axis. The outer circle, which moves at the fastest rate, is called "Ephemeral History." (We might also use the words "temporary" or "transitory" to describe this circle; it often refers to material-history items such as invitations, program brochures, or decorations used in a certain era.) Ideas move quickly into this circle, then migrate into the next circle or spin out of the model altogether. Applied to music, this includes new pieces that gain quick and immediate popularity, then either disappear or move to the next circle. Doran's example is the popular religious song "Seek ye first." This tune has existed since only 1972, a life that is too short to indicate whether it will remain in the permanent repertory. Of course, it has already appeared in several denominational hymnals, which may, in itself, qualify it for the second wheel in the Schillebeeckx model.

Before moving to that wheel, it might be helpful to hear the wisdom of Betty Carr Pulkingham, a classically trained leader in church music who has strongly influenced the development of popular religious song (hereafter, "PRS"). Dr. Pulkingham advises "that PRS not appear prematurely in hardbound hymnals, but that use of hymnal supplements and songbooks be encouraged as a proving-ground for such material."[5] She gives two solid reasons: (1) These songs have not yet proven themselves, and many of them will have a short shelf life. That is, some of them are very popular, but their appeal wears thin, and their effectiveness wanes. (2) Putting them in a hardback book suggests to many people that they are part of the standard repertoire.[6] Because they appear in an "official hymnal," seemingly approved by some regulatory body, people sing them regularly and may avoid looking for newer PRS. These songs are probably best published in temporary collections, unless through time they move to the next circle on the chart. Such a short lifespan does not imply that these PRS have no value. To the contrary, they may prove enormously effective in the short run—and unless we sing them, we will never find out if their value warrants moving into the next circle.

This second wheel is called "Conjectural History." (We might also use the words "hypothetical" or "suppositional" to describe this circle.) This body of music has outlasted the short lifespan of the music in the first wheel. Such a composition may well move to the permanent repertory of the church's music, but more time is needed to know this for sure. For many denominations the hymn "Lift high the cross" (tune: *Crucifer*) falls into this category. This fine hymn has rapidly gained popularity, appears in many major hymnals, and is sung often, especially at grand events in the church's life. In the long sweep of history, "Lift high the cross" is still a rather young entry, appearing only in 1916. Yet its strong impact would lead us to "conjecture" that it will enter the standard repertory. Only time will tell.

Sometimes a hymn is so quickly accepted that it seems a classic from the beginning. I recall a woman in my parish some years ago who commented on a hymn she loved. We had just purchased our denomination's new hymnal when she approached me, exclaiming, "Thank goodness they didn't take 'This joyful Eastertide' out of our hymnal! It's one of my favorites." In truth this hymn had never been included in a previous edition of an Episcopal hymnal. Although our parish had sung it from paperback hymnal supplements, this was the first hymnal of our denomination ever to include "This joyful Eastertide" (tune: *Vruechten*). Because she and I were dashing around between Sunday services and didn't have time for a full discussion, I simply replied, "Yes, I'm glad it's in the new hymnal, too."

The inside circle of Schillibeeckx's model is labeled "Structural History." Hymns that enter this wheel have become part of the structure of the church; they are so woven into the fabric of religious experience that it would be difficult to imagine congregational worship life without them. Examples of such hymns would include "O God, our help in ages past," (tune: *St. Anne*), "A mighty fortress is our God" (tune: *Ein' feste Burg*), and "Amazing grace" (tune: *Nettleton*).

Naturally denominations differ as to which hymns fit into the three categories. Perhaps denominations have more agreement about hymns in the Structural circle, but even here there are differences of opinion. Such disagreement is to be expected and doesn't distract from the helpful scheme of this model.

But here is a crucial aspect of the Schillibeeckx-Doran model: Every hymn that appears in the inner, Structural circle *began* in the outer, Ephemeral circle. We may feel that the classic hymns of Christianity have simply existed forever, but there was a point when they were new, untested by time, and dwelt among the temporary repertoire of the church.

Many of our hymn tunes came from sources well outside the church walls and were adapted for Christian usage: Such music as Bach's tune for "O sacred head" and the Irish folk tune *Slane* to which we sing "Be thou my vision" or "Lord of all hopefulness" began this way. While we generally have an easier time distinguishing between sacred and secular in the texts, when it comes to the musical setting, the line between them is vague and indistinct. Music that enters the church's repertoire (in the Ephemeral circle) often comes directly from nonchurch sources. Such an origin does not make these tunes in the least unworthy or ineffective. God is glorified by all creation. Some of our best, most beloved tunes first knew a vital life outside the church.

Schillibeeckx-Doran's model is an important foundation for our discussion, establishing the perspective that the church's music repertoire is dynamic, not static. There is and always has been movement, change. New music continually appears in the Ephemeral circle, gradually moves to the Conjectural circle (or disappears), and then, if it lasts, to the Structural circle. In light of this wisdom, we can't assume that the traditional music we now cherish has always existed, nor can we exclude new music that may initially challenge our ears and souls.

Understanding the Dilemma of Classical Musicians

To say that classically trained musicians are sensitive and vulnerable around the issue of PRS is putting it lightly. There are many simple, even obvious, reasons why this should be true.

Becoming a competent classical musician takes years of work. Whereas one can decide in one's late teens, or even early twenties, to become, say, a neurosurgeon, this is much too late in life to begin preparation for a career in music. Typically music study for future musicians begins by age six or seven with piano lessons. Parents invest precious dollars in private lessons, which is above and beyond the cost of a general education. Youngsters often have to neglect other childhood activities in order to acquire musical skills. This training continues, of course, in college and often in graduate school. Only a deep passion for classical music compels people to enter it as a vocation. Very few of those who invest this time and money will reap much of a lucrative reward. Many, of course, abandon music as a profession, even after years of preparation, because there are more easily acquired skills that yield greater financial rewards. Still, many persist.

After all this time, money, and practice, to sense that the existence of something the classical musician loves is threatened by PRS (especially if imposed without mutual agreement among church leaders) is unthinkable. The perceived danger is that PRS will supplant classical music in the church's repertoire. How can something so cherished as classical music, for which not only the child but also the entire family has sacrificed, face a potential demise? To the musician this seems a threat to the very core of his or her being.

The threat has some reality, because many churches have abandoned their heritage of classical music for the easier vocabulary in PRS. These quickly learned, easily assimilated songs find their way into a congregation's repertoire more readily than classical hymns, or any music that requires more concentration, more repeated use before taking root. This is not surprising. Anyone who has raised children knows that teaching children to eat hearty, nutritious dishes takes more effort than light, sweet foods.

Performing music in popular styles sometimes can seem beneath her dignity to the classical musician. Popular music may well lack the subtlety, nuance, and sophistication of classical music.

After years of luxuriating in classical music with its sometimes complex, refined construction, the classical musician frequently feels that PRS sells the congregation short. ("How ya gonna keep 'em down on the farm after they've seen Paree?" asked a World War I song.7) Of course, there are exceptions in sacred "popular" music as well as secular. One reason that so many classical musicians love the music of Broadway composer Stephen Sondheim, for example, is that it has much of the musical depth of classical music. Nonetheless, the contrast persists.

Some classical musicians grow up with a love of popular music and perform it alongside the classical music that is their primary passion. A few musicians even pay their way through music school by performing popular music. These are musicians who don't get caught in stylistic conflict. They accept the contrasts simply as different artistic expressions. For others, the contrasting styles constitute sworn enemies, making an issue of one's loyalty. In addition to these musicians, there are others who, though quite content to enjoy (or even perform) popular music, draw the line when it comes to a service of worship. Such reasoning goes: "Popular music is okay for dances or for concerts in sports arenas, but music for worship needs to have dignity, depth, refinement."

Classically trained musicians feel under assault by the prevailing American culture. For a couple of generations, we have witnessed the steady erosion of music education in the public schools, ostensibly justified by budget constraints. This has resulted in a populace more illiterate about music than the other arts. For example, a well-educated person in our culture is expected to have a basic grasp of the work of Shakespeare, at least to the extent of recognizing the names of the plays. Yet, in many instances, the same person could not name a single composition by Mozart, an artist of equal importance in the history of Western Europe. To the extent this is true, it is a severe shortcoming of our education system.

Some churches have maintained a steady use of classical music in their services. In such parishes the congregation sings classical hymns of the faith (like "Praise to the Lord, the almighty" to the tune *Lobe den Herren*), the choir sings classical anthem literature (like "Ave verum corpus" by Mozart), and the organist plays classical organ music (like the preludes and fugues of J. S. Bach), along with modern music in the classical tradition (such as compositions by Benjamin Britten, Aaron Copland, Alice Parker, Jane Marshall, or Arvo Pärt). In other churches, however, classical music is seldom if ever used, having been replaced by music in popular styles (so-called "folk" music or rock). For those who love the traditional music of the church, hearing it considered "irrelevant" by some of today's Christians is alarming.

For anyone to think that the great music in our cultural legacy will simply disappear (due to current popular preferences) is short-sighted indeed. This would be akin to a notion that popular television shows, no matter how excellent, will replace Shakespeare plays. Just as we can be reasonably sure *The Tempest* will be appreciated for centuries to come, so we can assume that Mozart, including the great sacred compositions, will endure the changes in both culture and church. Indeed, the church at various points in history has been the major repository of learning and the preserver of cultural masterpieces. In *How the Irish Saved Civilization*, author Thomas Cahill demonstrates how monks saved the treasures of classical civilization from the time of the fall of Rome (fifth century AD) to the rise of Charlemagne (crowned 800 AD).[8] In the same way the church through much of its history has championed and preserved classical music.

While it is true that the preservation of classical music is not the church's primary mission, trained musicians nevertheless have a valid commission that needs to be heard and recognized: It is reckless and wasteful for churches to abandon the vast heritage of great sacred music, attempting to make its worship services seem musically "relevant." In many cases the great classics of sacred music have sprung from the rich soil of spiritual encounter. The heritage classical musicians defend and are called to represent has not only led to much enjoyment of soul over the centuries, but it also has fostered deep religious experience. To be sure, the quality of workmanship has guaranteed its longevity, but, just as sure, classical music has led many people to faith and discipleship.

Classical Musicians' Expanding Appreciation

Conflicts between clergy who yearn for greater diversity of musical styles—loosening up the kinds of musical choices—and musicians who are intractable on this point have been known to produce open conflict and the severing of employment contracts. However much we may crave parity in the relationship between clergy and musicians, this fact remains certain: Clergy are usually the employers or supervisors of church musicians. In an outright struggle for power, few musicians prevail. The church is at its worst in battles for personal dominance, so naturally it is preferable that such contests be avoided altogether. Our vocational calling would prove its depth and substance if the church were to model fair and equitable employment practice rather than lagging behind our secular counterparts, as is so often the case. A clear understanding at the time of employment is one way of dodging this bullet. But what of situations where musicians have already established long tenures? In many such cases the musician has deep connections to the faith community, and is dearly beloved by the parish. Is there a way to defuse this bomb?

First, it is instructive to acknowledge that the label "classical church music" is not monolithic; it is already diverse. Analyze the contents of even the most traditional of hymnals, such as *Hymns Ancient and Modern* (whose 1861 and 1875 editions became the prototype of the modern hymnal)[9] and the *Hymnal 1940* (which widely influenced subsequent books), and you notice some disarming facts. These hymnals contain folk music, Genevan psalm-settings, American hymns, German chorales, English cathedral music, French carols, chant, and tunes taken from secular sources, to mention a few styles.

Hymnals today continue to expand in the variety of music considered appropriate for Christian worship, but even the older hymn-books cited above include diverse materials. We have come to view them as classics, but the editors at the time were breaking new ground. Some of their innovations faltered, but others became standard hymnody. While the editors were concerned with preserving the best of accepted hymnody, they also embraced experimentation and innovation. Has this process ceased, or does hymn repertoire continue to expand?

The last half of the twentieth century witnessed a remarkable explosion of new hymns that continues in our time. New hymn texts and tunes have proliferated at an astounding rate. Inevitably many new creations have fallen (or will fall) by the wayside, but many have found their way into new hymnals. How critical it is to remember that our current repertoire of hymns is as rich as it is because we remained open to experimentation.

The Valuable Counsel of Trained Musicians

One of the solutions to clergy's dilemma when classical musicians resist using PRS is to put someone else in charge of it. But this provides a temporary truce at best. One may hear from the principal parish musician, "Oh, we have that kind of music in my parish, but, thank God, I have nothing to do with it." Contrast that with the following story. A leading church musician in this country was approached by his clergy leader, who was trying to be sensitive when she said, "We are going to try an occasional 'prayer and praise' service, but I want you to know that you don't have to be involved with it." The musician's answer may have surprised her. "If there is any music making on this campus, I'd like to be part of it."

This musician then set about trying to discover the best examples of this repertoire, looking for music that is theologically sound and has musical and textual merit. Then he assembled the best musicians the parish could muster and set about introducing a new style of music for this parish. After this new musical service had been in place for a while, I had the opportunity of worshipping at this parish. Never have I heard popular religious song presented with such musical substance, subtlety, and beauty. As is often the case, music was the primary determinant of style, and this was a remarkably effective worship service.

In the above case, the classically trained musician, though by this point a longtime practitioner of his art, was willing to learn and lead a new style of music. He brought to it the consummate skill of a lifetime of training and experience, producing an extraordinarily rich musical product and a superb worship service. To be sure, the parish continued its rich diet of classical music, but the musical menu of the congregation was expanded. Had this service been assigned to a musician with less training and experience, the results would have been quite different.

The above story need not imply that classical musicians are essential for effective presentations of different styles of music. Certainly wonderful performances of all kinds of music occur every day, often presented by musicians who know only one particular style of music. There is, however, a long tradition of classical musicians' incorporating elements of popular music in their music. Look at popular dance forms that J. S. Bach incorporated into his suites, such as the *gavotte*, the *sarabande*, or the *courante*. Likewise, Claude Debussy employed the African American dance "cakewalk" in his piano composition "Golliwog's Cakewalk." English composer Ralph Vaughan Williams traveled the English countryside with primitive recording equipment to collect folk songs sung only in rural areas at that time. Subsequently, he incorporated into his music the tunes and styles he gleaned from this experience, greatly enhancing his quality as a composer. One wonders, in fact, if many of these folk tunes (as well as the dance forms cited above) didn't escape extinction by finding their way into classical and even sacred compositions.

Alternatives to PRS—World Music

In some local situations PRS may be entirely inappropriate. At the same time, the leaders may wish to introduce genuine folk music. By this we mean music that is created by anonymous composers, arising from a national or cultural group, as opposed to music written by a single composer in folk style for commercial publication or recording. For example, "If I had a hammer" was composed in 1949 by Pete Seeger and Lee Hays. Although it is in a recognizable folk style, it would not qualify as folk music, like "O Shenandoah," whose origin is impossible to trace. The latter was created by some anonymous tunesmith and probably altered by succeeding performers through the years.

Those who wish to broaden the musical repertoire of their congregations, and especially those who wish to attract people from a wide range of cultures and nationalities, will find increasingly available songs for worship from a wide variety of cultural contexts. In recent years music from various sub-Saharan African countries, South America, Asia, the Pacific Islands, and other sources have gained remarkable popularity among congregations. Songs like "Siyahamba" ("We are marching in the light of God") from South Africa, for example, have rapidly become a staple in the musical repertoire of congregations of several denominations.

Learning such "world music" or "global music," as it is called, opens us to the worship experience of Christians who are separated from us geographically and culturally. When people of a dominant culture sing the music of a minority culture, a powerful message of unity is voiced. Singing global music can also be very welcoming to visitors from other countries. Two experiences bear this out. A few years ago I visited South Africa with a delegation from my parish in an effort to establish some mission work there. While traveling on the bus through the beautiful countryside, we learned a couple of songs, the Zulu song "Siyahamba," described above, and a very popular folk song in Xhosa (the "clicking" language). When we arrived at our destinations and were warmly greeted by native speakers of these languages, we began to sing these songs. The extraordinary delight of our hosts is nearly impossible to describe, as they heard foreigners trying (however poorly) to sing local songs in local languages. Hardly had we begun to sing before they joined us in hearty singing. Only when asked did they offer good-natured advice about our pronunciation. Such a modest effort on our part demonstrated the common bond in faith we all shared, giving us instant ties of friendship with these African Christians.

The second story is when a delegation of South Africans visited our church in Washington, D.C. We had spent several months preparing music for the service that incorporated folk songs and church music from their country. We knew that this was risky, that we were taking the chance of offending our guests, because we might easily have gotten it all wrong. Knowing the immense graciousness of the South African people, however, gave us hope that they might be thrilled to hear music from home. The risk we took was worth the effort at hospitality. As it happened, African bodies began to move and hands began to clap within seconds after our singing commenced.

There are several sources for songs of worship from other cultures. *Halle, Halle: We Sing the World Around*, edited by Michael Hawn, published by Choristers' Guild, offers a rich sampling of church music from around the world.[10] There is background information on the individual songs, as well as a pronunciation guide to the languages. A demonstration recording is also available. Hawn has developed a reputation for his travels around the world, collecting, editing and publishing songs from disparate cultures. Several other books by this author delve into the riches of global music.

The General Board of Global Ministries of the United Methodist Church, which is headquartered in New York City, also publishes several volumes of music from around the world under the series name "Global Praise."[11] They make available a music resources catalog that lists a number of print collections of global music, as well as recordings.

Clergy and musicians who want to open their parishioners' minds and hearts to Christians from around the world, and enrich the repertoire of the local congregation, will find global music an attractive alternative (or addition) to commercially produced popular song. In several parish settings, as well as seminary chapel, I have had the delight of observing people, with little exposure to music from cultures beyond their own, enthusiastically singing international music. Even in instances where the leaders had trepidations about any potential response—places where nothing like this had ever been attempted—the results were overwhelmingly positive.

Alternatives to PRS—Two Religious Communities

In addition to global or world music, two religious communities— Taizé, in France, and Iona, in Scotland—have created worship music in a singable, folk style that captures the imagination of Christians around the world.

The Taizé Community was begun in 1940 in a tiny French village by a young man named Roger Louis Schütz-Marsauche, from the Protestant tradition. This young man, who became known as simply Brother Roger of Taizé, was soon joined by other brothers, and an ecumenical monastic community formed, comprising both

Protestants and Catholics. Over the years increasing numbers of young people began to appear at Taizé, journeying there on pilgrimage to seek the spiritual light and transformation the community had created—its "parable of community." When I visited there, the brothers welcomed what they considered a relatively small number of pilgrims, meaning three thousand. In the summers, we were told, a week's visitors often numbered eight thousand.

The community developed its own style of worship, characterized by abundant silence and prayer through music. Much of the music was composed by a Parisian church musician named Jacques Berthier, though he was seldom credited in publications. The brothers sent texts to Monsieur Berthier, which he set in simple tunes with rich but easily performed harmony. Sometimes these were preexisting folk tunes, but, more often, they were newly created by Berthier.

Many of the texts were in Latin, because the community discovered that an increasingly international body of pilgrims could easily assimilate the limited vowel sounds of that language. At the same time, efforts were made to accommodate whatever the language of the majority of pilgrims at any given time.

Taizé "chants" (or "songs," the words being indistinguishable in French) are typically short, simple, and are repeated many times. After a number of repetitions, the singer begins to notice a deepening of the impact of the chant, as one is drawn more fully into prayer.

In the last two decades, an increasing number of North American young people have visited the community of Taizé. The accommodations are Spartan—often a sleeping bag or a tent suffice—but the hospitality is rich. Along with worship three times a day, pilgrims are offered Bible teaching in small groups, divided by language.[12]

Many churches around the world have initiated services in the style of Taizé, while others have incorporated the meditative, often hauntingly beautiful songs into their own customary forms of worship. Often parishes that wish to stretch their musical repertoire beyond traditional hymnody and service music, but for whom popular religious song is not a viable option, find the music of Taizé an attractive alternative.

During communion these chants can be particularly effective. Because of the movement necessary while taking communion, people may find it difficult to also shuffle the hymnal. Taizé chants are so short that they can be easily memorized. If the same chant is done for a liturgical season (or for several weeks), the congregation comes to know it by heart, singing it before and after taking communion.

Perhaps the most powerful testimonies about the power of these simple, attractive songs come from parishioners. In one case a woman said, "I was struggling with sleep, agonizing over some problems facing me. Suddenly that song we've been singing during communion came to me. It ushered me into a quiet, prayerful place in my heart, and soon I was asleep."

Perhaps nothing would please the founders of Taizé more than to know that these sung invocations, often addressed directly to God, have brought people into prayer. Taizé chants (and recordings) are published by the community in France and distributed in the U.S. by GIA Publications, Chicago. At Taizé, instruments brought by pilgrims are incorporated into worship (and published parts are made available), but the primary texture of the songs is vocal, kept intentionally simple to include everyone.

Another ecumenical religious community that has developed its own music is the Iona Community, named for the island off the coast of Scotland where it is located.

The Iona Community was founded in Glasgow and Iona in 1938 by George MacLeod, minister, visionary, and prophetic witness for peace, in the context of the poverty and despair of the Depression. From a dockland parish in Govan, Glasgow, MacLeod took unemployed skilled craftsmen and young trainee clergy to Iona to rebuild both the monastic quarters of the medieval abbey and the shared common life by working and living together, sharing skills and effort as well as joys and achievement. That original task became a sign of hopeful rebuilding of community in Scotland and beyond. The experience shaped—and continues to shape—the practice and principles of the Iona Community.[13]

Iona is a tiny and beautiful Hebridean island off the west coast of Scotland, the cradle of Christianity in Scotland, where in 563 AD the Irish monk Columba (Columkille) established a monastic settlement that evangelized large parts of Scotland and the north of England and became an important center of European Christianity. In the Middle Ages it became the site of a Benedictine abbey, and over the centuries it has attracted many thousands of people on their own pilgrim journeys.[14]

The songs of Iona bear some similarities to those of Taizé. They tend to be simple, with few words, offering themselves to multiple repetitions. Many of the songs are by John L. Bell, some in collaboration with fellow Iona Community member Graham Maule. Bell is an ordained minister of the Church of Scotland and a member of the Iona Community.

If the information on Iona is briefer than that on Taizé, it is only because I have not had the pleasure of visiting there. The songs are attractive, practical, and, like those of Taizé, draw worshipers into a place of prayer and meditation. They are published by the community in Scotland under its imprint Wild Goose Publications. Like the music of Taizé, the printed music and recordings of the Iona Community are distributed in the U.S. by GIA Publications, Chicago.

Some church leaders who find that popular religious song simply doesn't work in the contexts of their worship may discover the need for simple, prayerful, folklike songs met in the music of Taizé and Iona. Naturally one need not exclude the other, and some churches will choose both PRS and music from these communities.

Congregational Segregation by Music Style

Clergy implement another practice in trying to avoid a conflict between contrasting musical styles: separating the congregation into different music styles. Once again, I appeal to no less an authority than Betty Carr Pulkingham.[15] She strongly recommends against dividing the congregation into "traditional" and "contemporary" styles. The operative word "divide" signals that this practice is something that should be avoided. Sometimes a serious division in the parish is the terrible result from such a well-intentioned effort.

Liturgy at its best is like a family meal, rich with hospitality and the deep connections that result. When planning a family reunion, would we schedule separate seatings for people based on their preference for different kinds of foods? If the larger concern is the family's being together, we will tend to endure minor disagreements over the menu. Here is crazy Uncle Elmer, who loves giblets and drinks buttermilk with cornbread crumbled in it, and there is young Wanda, who doesn't really come alive until the strawberry rhubarb pie is served. While we could avoid the discomfort of family members who don't want to eat each other's favorite dish (or even be in the same room with those who do), our devotion to family trumps all differences in taste. We endure what may seem the eccentricities of others for the sake of family unity. Sometimes a good laugh will bless the meal, but at other times someone may discover a strange dish that becomes oddly palatable.

At our worst, congregations reflect the rank consumerism of American society, demanding what suits our tastes and satisfies our particular appetites. At our best, we delight in the joy of being together in the rich, varied, and nourishing presence of God's Spirit.

CHAPTER FIVE

Music Ministry with Children

Git on board, little chillen,
Git on board, little chillen,
Git on board, little chillen,
There's room for many a more.

A complete parish music ministry includes children. While it used to be commonplace to consider children the church of the future, most church leaders now know this thinking is specious. Children are in every sense part of the church of today. In fact, we may be certain that unless we insure that children are the church of today, they are unlikely to be the church of tomorrow.

Any congregation is incomplete without children, because their witness of joy and life is essential. They are an integral component, a vital piece of the picture, a key ingredient without which the Body of Christ is incomplete. When Jesus instructed the disciples not to forbid children to come to him (Mark 10:14), he wasn't addressing the church of the future. Rather, he named children the exemplary citizens in the reign of God.

Bring Your Finest Gifts

For a parish to enjoy a vital ministry of music with children, it needs to employ the finest resources it can—the strongest leaders, best facilities, and choicest music equipment and materials. This is not said to discourage parishes whose resources are limited; we know the most important ingredients are the nonmaterial ones— time, attention, and love. But we need to share with children whatever abundance God has given us rather than expend our best only on the adult participants in music. The results of such a strong commitment can be extraordinary. Because young minds are so absorbent, so malleable, they respond quickly and dramatically, producing musical and spiritual growth that is immediately evident as it grows to fruition in children's lives and the life of the church.

One frequently encounters adult parishioners who can recall music they learned in preschool choirs. For example, I can still sing the Spanish words to the chorus of "Jesus Loves Me," taught to me as a four-year-old in Greenwood, Mississippi. This phenomenon of adult parishioners' remembering songs from childhood demonstrates the two superb benefits of that experience: First, they are still in church. Contributing to the worship of the church and learning the great music of its heritage can implant lifelong patterns of commitment to and spiritual attachment with the church. Second, what they learned as choir children has stayed with them, has become an integral part of their being.

Children Learn to Be Taken Seriously

Children are, of course, fully capable of making a serious contribution to the liturgy of the parish, one that brings blessings to the children themselves and to the entire congregation. This is visible when children have been taught to regard themselves as regular leaders of worship rather than performers ushered into the worship service for an occasional entertainment. Even parents can learn the importance of children's thorough integration into worship and can come to prefer this over parading them into the service for coos and applause.

An excellent music minister to children taught me that one of the worst things adults can do to children is to make them cute.[1] This is not to disparage those occasions when children are spontaneously adorable. Who (including this doting grandfather) doesn't enjoy that? But it is important to discourage the intentional design of situations to elicit the response "cute." Children readily differentiate between being condescended to and being respected. It is entirely possible to find enjoyment (and even fun) with them in music that has theological integrity and artistic merit through treating their contribution to worship as important and substantive. When young people sing fine music and present it in a manner that enriches worship, there are untold benefits. Once we demonstrate to children that their role in worship is serious, they will never again be satisfied to be treated as a diverting cameo appearance.

This is true not only with regard to the manner in which young people participate in worship; the quality of the repertoire we choose for them also demonstrates the importance we give children's contribution to worship.

Two stories will illustrate. Some years ago in an active music ministry for young people, we somehow developed an annual tradition of singing a marvelous motet by Palestrina, especially appropriate to the Scripture readings during Lent.[2] One year, as this music was distributed in girl choir rehearsal, I heard a loud gasp from a young singer. I winced, expecting to hear a disparaging remark that might influence other singers' attitude negatively. Oh, me of little faith. What followed the gasp, in fact, was an exclamatory, "I love this piece!" The astounding leadership strength of this young girl would fully manifest itself a few years hence, but even then she had a strong influence with her peers. Suddenly the entire choir discovered that this piece was cool. I uttered a silent prayer: "Thanks be to God. I can die a happy man. Children can love the great music of the church's heritage."

The second story involves a choir of older teenagers. A new musician had come to assist me with the leadership of this choir. When he selected a certain trivial piece of music, I had some trepidation about the reaction of the youth choir. They had grown up in a choir-training program featuring music of substance and merit, and the composition he had chosen was at best playful—light by comparison. Nevertheless, it was his turn to conduct, mine to accompany, and I decided it was only fair to accord him freedom to perform what he had chosen.

This choir comprised teenagers who were typical of their generation. For example, the music they listened to between choir rehearsals was not anything I particularly relished. While they could be a rambunctious group, they were also respectful of adult leadership, and so for the first two weeks they said nothing about the music my colleague had chosen. On the third week, however, there was a sudden, unexpected eruption from one of the kindest, most gracious members of the choir. Dramatically throwing the music to the choir room floor, he expostulated: "Could we please sing some real church music?" We all had a good laugh, including the new leader, and the piece was put aside.

I hasten to add that not all music they sang was somber-toned or classical in style. As is evident throughout this book, I ascribe to a wide diversity of music, spanning various cultures, periods, and rhythmic styles. The point of the two stories is that these young people had had a rich and substantial musical menu that cultivated in them the expectation of being taken seriously as musicians.

Offer a Nutritious Musical Diet

A musical diet is comparable with a food diet. It needs to be varied and delicious, but also nutritious. While I like cotton candy as much as anyone, and wouldn't forbid a child from eating it, I would be a poor parent indeed if I let him think this was nourishing food and could be his main diet. Light music, like light food, often has immediate appeal, titillating singers and listeners alike, but its effect is inevitably short-lived. With music of depth we take longer to develop our appreciation, absorbing its beauty after repeated exposures, and our enjoyment of it is likely to be sustained over a longer time. It bears repetition. Indeed, our appreciation of such music grows with familiarity. It is thus more likely to lodge in the permanent repertoire of both parish and individual singer.

In the cases of the two choirs cited above, these young people saw themselves not only as musicians. They knew they were making weekly musical contributions to the worship life of the parish, so that when even the youngest among them was asked about the chorister's role, the unwavering response was: "To lead worship." Contrast this with the tempting but reductive practice of showcasing young choirs, front and center, in a manner that provokes laughter and elicits applause. One approach is exploitative; the other is respectful.

A respectful music ministry for young people seems countercultural in many respects. It is countercultural for most young people to attend church regularly. It is also countercultural for them to work voluntarily and harmoniously with adult leaders. It is countercultural that while enmeshed in the latest sound clips, downloaded from the Internet, they also find a place in their hearts for the heritage of the church's greatest music.

Moving to Fine Music for Youth

How do we get from here to there? How do we transform music ministry with children from cute performances to significant liturgical contribution? How do we present music that enriches the corporate life of the parish and touches deeply the lives of those who make the music, as well as those who hear it?

First of all, we start with the youngest—preschoolers and elementary age children. At these young ages children, like sponges, are able to absorb new teaching effortlessly. They are vigorous learners and enthusiastic about accomplishing goals set by adult leaders. Later, when the desperate need for peer approval arises, they are likely to be more cooperative with adults if patterns have already been assimilated. Often teenage singers succeed because they have begun singing in choirs at the elementary or middle school stage. The values, absorbed in early childhood, persist: that they are highly esteemed contributors to the worship life of the parish, that they can be trusted with the best music available, that adults take them seriously as human beings, moreover, as fellow members of the Body of Christ.

How do clergy encourage this commitment to music with children? First, by engaging music leaders who affirm these values. If such leaders can't be found, clergy will need to cultivate them and contribute to their formation.

Finding Help from Professionals

Fortunately there are organizations that can be immensely helpful in developing a great music ministry with children. Chiefly, the Royal School of Church Music (RSCM) has a long and successful track record in the training of young choristers. Founded in the U.K. in 1927, RSCM is now an international, ecumenical organization working actively in many countries, including the United States. RSCM helps leaders establish goals and standards, practices that produce the highest caliber music work with children.

Its mission statement spells out the Royal School of Church Music program: It seeks to serve churches by:

- encouraging music making in general, and singing in particular;

- providing training in essential skills for church music;

- developing understanding of music in the church's ministry and worship;

- encouraging good music everywhere through fostering outreach from the churches into the community;

- engaging with young people in singing.[3]

Unfortunately in many parish music programs, children learn choral literature "by rote." This means that a choir director sings or plays their melodic line, and the children repeat it. Expert choir trainer John Bertalot says, "'Rote' is a four-letter word."[4] The problem with this shortcut is that it discourages children from learning to read music. Music reading is a skill that opens new vistas to young singers, enabling them to grasp music quickly and thoroughly. The RSCM program establishes in children a comprehensive musicianship base along with developing their vocal facility. Youngsters who spend several years in an RSCM program emerge with impressive music skills. They also know the liturgy and theology of their church and the place of music in worship.

In an RSCM program young people work to accomplish specific tasks laid out in a comprehensive curriculum.[5] As they develop in musicianship, vocal ability, and leadership in worship, they advance from one stage to another, designated by the award of different-colored ribbons for their level of achievement. These ribbons are worn around the neck and over choir vestments, each bearing the bronze insignia of the Royal School of Church Music. Much as in scouting or karate classes, these symbolic items mark their progress.

The ribbons are highly prized, and children feel a great sense of accomplishment when they receive ribbons that indicate successively higher goals. A short ceremony, conducted during a Sunday morning liturgy at the end of each academic year, indicates an advance in skill. Observing this ceremony in the context of worship not only firmly connects the choristers' work to the liturgy of the church, it also involves the parish community in an important ceremonial recognition of these young people. Everyone takes pleasure in praising their youthful accomplishments throughout the year's worship.

Although it was begun in the Anglican Church and transplanted to the Episcopal Church in the U.S. and other Anglican churches around the world, the RSCM is now thoroughly ecumenical. The broad principles of its style of organization and instruction are applicable to the work of many denominations.

In addition to supporting choristers' work at the local parish level, RSCM also offers marvelous regional summer courses. Young people who are ready for such a challenge can attend weeklong events where the music is rehearsed under dynamic music directors who have been carefully selected for their effectiveness in working with youth.

Services are prepared, and worship is offered each day. Often there is a culminating festival service on a Sunday morning or Sunday afternoon. These services are impressive in their beauty and power, a public demonstration of the week's remarkable accomplishments. For young persons whose training in the parish music ministry has prepared them for this thorough experience, they meet like-minded young colleagues from around the country, sharing their love for participating in great sacred music in a worship setting.

For more information about the Royal School of Church Music, go to their website (http://www.rscmamerica.org). There, clergy will discover how the parish can become a member of RSCM, how the musician can get training in this approach to choir training, and what courses are offered for young people. Some of the finest children's music making on the planet occurs under the auspices of the RSCM, and its leaders are always looking for ways to involve more music programs in this important work.

Urge Your Parish to Envision a Significant Music Ministry with Youth

Music ministry with children takes a great deal of planning and effort, but the results more than outweigh the expended energy. Young people are affirmed in their ministry of leading worship, develop invaluable music skills, and are bonded to the church community in a relationship that can last for a lifetime. When clergy tell me that they don't have enough children to develop this ministry, I respond that three children can easily make a choir. Furthermore, if you are trying to attract children and their families to your parish, there is no better way than to provide a quality music ministry with children.

A colleague tells the moving story of a mother who stopped by the church office to say that their family was being transferred to another town. Her delightful middle-school-aged son had enjoyed the music program at the church for several years, making it difficult for the family to leave the community. Clearly showing emotion in her face, she said to the music director, "Thank you for caring so much for my child." The church musician was immensely grateful that all the planning, scheduling, and organization in the program led to this end: The mother felt that her child had been deeply cared for.

CHAPTER SIX

Music for Funerals and Weddings

Swing low, sweet chariot,
Comin' for to carry me home;
Swing low, sweet chariot,
Comin' for to carry me home.

Oh, I'm a-gonna sing, gonna sing,
Gonna sing all along the way,
Oh, I'm a-gonna sing, gonna sing,
Gonna sing all along the way.

It is easy to understand why church professionals are leery of weddings and funerals for nonparishioners. Sometimes those who don't appreciate the nature and function of the church can become downright abusive when planning weddings and funerals. As is true in many instances, however, there is an opportunity behind this challenge. People do approach the church for ministry at the most important and vulnerable points in their lives—birth, baptism, conflict, illness, weddings, and funerals. How the church handles such occasions may well determine whether the present need has simply been met, leading to no further interaction, or people are drawn more deeply into the life of the church.

Because of negative experiences, some parishes have a policy that the church performs weddings or officiates funerals only for members of the congregation. Still, other parishes feel strongly that churches are called to serve those outside our walls, and that, moreover, an opportunity for evangelism often presents itself when offering ministry to families on such occasions. Sometimes at this moment of vulnerability, people examine their lives and discover that their spiritual garden needs tending.

Weddings and funerals are also an opportunity to minister to people beyond the families themselves. The service may be filled with people who have no strong, current connection with a church. Like the families, based on the experience of this worship service, they may come to sense that there is something missing in their lives that the church can fill. If the liturgy and music are done with care, and if they are typical of the parish's usual services, those in attendance may be drawn to the church. Nothing establishes the tone of the service like music. If it is done well and if it is similar in character to the regular worship of the parish, people may be inclined to return for worship.

Music for Funerals

There is no doubt that *someone* will establish a policy for music at funerals. If the clergy and musicians don't do it, then each family that approaches the church for a service will feel free to establish whatever policy they wish. This might very well include items that clergy feel violate the theology of the church or at least the spirit of the service. At a time of bereavement, pastoral treatment of the family is of the utmost importance, naturally guiding all plans and decisions. At the same time, wise clergy and musicians will have standards firmly in mind. Unlike planning for weddings, where policies are published and distributed in advance (see below), the death of a loved one is not the best time to send out directives. Still, there are customs and standards that are important.

It is sometimes good to lay a foundation at the beginning of the discussion of music for the service, establishing guidelines gently but clearly. For example, one might say, "As we begin to discuss the music for your father's service, I wonder if I might offer some guidelines that will help us in planning. The funeral service is an Easter liturgy and music focused on the resurrection will set that tone. Everything we do will demonstrate that this is a service of worship." Sometimes this avoids your having to say no to a request for something you deem inappropriate. Even if members of the family have arrived with suggestions of inappropriate music, this gentle guide may cause them to rethink the request, avoiding embarrassment. Many churches have a firm policy, for example, that no secular music is allowed in the funeral or memorial service. Hearing clergy explain the guideline that everything we do will be appropriate for a service of worship may deter requests before they are voiced.

Every church musician or clergy who has done funerals for years has stories of outlandish requests. Usually the humor of the situation can't be fully appreciated until the occasion has passed, but a light touch is helpful. For example, I once had a call from a bishop who wished to discuss the music for his sister's funeral. His major request was to have "Hawaiian Wedding Song," popularized by Elvis Presley, sung as a solo. I followed my first instinct, which was to say, "Bishop, I don't know that piece, and I'm sure I can't learn it in time for the funeral." Neither of these statements was exactly true. My clergyperson, upon hearing this, responded with a wink, "My son, you did the right thing. You are absolved of your sin."

You may find it helpful that you and the musician procure or develop a template for planning the service. Having this in hand while meeting with the family will simplify things. Below are some suggestions for guidelines for funeral music, which may need to be adapted to the particular denomination or parish. Again, these guidelines are offered as a reference for clergy and musicians, not as rules and regulations to be given to grieving families.

- The funeral/memorial service is a service of worship, and the musical elements will be appropriate to a service of worship.

- This is an Easter liturgy, and the music will reflect that. Music that pulls the friends and family into a state of despair is avoided; music that builds them up and offers them consolation and hope is encouraged.

- It is usually best that music not be done by family members or close friends who are grieving, but rather by those who are in a position to minister to them. When a family member attempts to sing and breaks down, this is likely to be what people remember most about the service.

- Many people for whom church is not a familiar experience will be in the service. Because of this, hymns that are familiar across denominational lines are preferable. The immediate family may include several denominational traditions, in which case it is pastorally sensitive to seek hymns from those traditions as well as those of the parish.

- Sometimes family members will have ideas about hymns. Often parishes keep a record of hymns parishioners would like sung at their funerals. In most instances, however, family members are at a complete loss for ideas. Most hymnals offer suggestions for funeral hymns, and it is good for the clergy and musician planning the service to have in mind some hymns to recommend.

- Music prior to the service is designed to help people become comfortable with the space and to prepare for the service.

Music that is quiet, sustained, and reflective is usually better than music that is loud, percussive, and declamatory.

- The very best musicians available should be engaged for the service, especially those who understand the nature and purpose of the service. Ideally people will remember the music not because it stood out (due to poor quality or because of excessive showiness), but because it was a vital element, supporting and enhancing the service.

- As was mentioned in the introductory remarks, people are often brought into the fuller life of the church because of a pastoral service. If the service reflects the best worship practice of the parish, and if it is done with care and sensitivity, people may choose to return for worship.

- If a choir or soloist(s) participate, their selections are carefully chosen for appropriateness. Music whose text is from Scripture or consonant with Scripture is preferable. Soloists, even seasoned ones, will usually need guidance as to what is appropriate.

- If there is music at the close of the service, it will be joyful and celebratory in nature, affirming the resurrection message.

- The minister or the church musician is well advised to have guidelines and boundaries committed to memory or notes available when planning the service with the family. At a time of grief, it is not appropriate to give people a published list of expectations. As was stated in the introduction to this chapter, laying out a few basic principles in advance of the conversation can avoid the embarrassment of requests that the minister or priest deems inappropriate.

- Music of a popular nature, significant to the deceased or the bereaved (Broadway tunes, love songs, folk songs, rock songs, school songs) is best saved for a reception in the home or the parish hall/fellowship hall.

- Above all, pastoral sensitivity in dealing with the family guides the entire planning session.

All this having been said, the final bullet trumps everything else. There have been occasions when I did music for a funeral that was less than ideal, because it seemed pastorally mandated by the situation. When to stand firm and when to bend can only be determined by the advice of a wise mentor and the guidance of the Holy Spirit.

Music for Weddings

Weddings vary greatly from one denomination to another, as well as from parish to parish. In some churches secular music is common. The most extreme example I have witnessed is an independent church, whose pastor felt that the wedding was a secular occasion, even though held at the church. Because of this philosophy, a wide gamut of music was allowed. The most interesting application of this principle was the wedding of a man from Georgia and a woman from South America. The processional was the Argentine national anthem, and the recessional was "Dixie."

In many churches, however, the wedding continues to be considered a service of worship, and this is reflected in the music. Secular music is best reserved for the reception, and, in fact, will probably be enjoyed more in that setting.

Published Guidelines and Music

In the above discussion of the choice of music for funerals, clergy were discouraged from burdening a grieving family with written guidelines. In wedding planning, however, exactly the opposite is best. Most parishes are likely to provide the couple with published guidelines, covering everything from fees to how the issue of photography and photographers is to be handled. (Unfortunately, past abuses are usually the impetus that creates such policies.) Thus it is both convenient and highly desirable to have guidelines about music in the same booklet.

Such suggestions will begin with the positive attributes of appropriate and effective music, rather than to open with what is not allowed. Then it is good to urge the couple to meet with the parish musician, suggesting that they arrange an appointment. Hurt and angry feelings are usually the result of couples who come with their minds already pretty set about the music they have thought they wanted before ever reading the guidelines or consulting with the clergy or parish musician. In the capable hands of a pastoral musician, couples can make wise decisions about their wedding music that reflect their own personal choices while remaining true to the parish context.

There are two critical areas where the couple and parish leadership need to come to terms: appropriate music and appropriate performers. With regard to the latter, parishes may vary between these two extremes: (1) Anyone the couple wants is allowed to perform at the wedding; (2) nobody except the parish musician or those engaged by the parish musician can perform. This can be a difficult area.

A couple may have a close friend or relative whom they want to sing or play for the service, and that person may or may not have the skills to do so—unfortunately, more often, they do not. The couple's view of this is naturally subjective, based upon feelings for the performer rather than musical judgment. Countless times I have participated in weddings where musicians invited by the family were embarrassing to everyone present.

Two stories illustrate. One was the case of the grandmother of the bride, who, much earlier in her life, had been a musician singing regularly. The grandmother herself tried gracefully and repeatedly to refuse the bride's request, but the bride was insistent. On the day of the wedding, the grandmother was so terrified about singing that she felt faint before and during the service. She was uncertain she would be able to stand, much less sing. The singing she produced was unsteady and barely audible. Through no fault of her own, the grandmother's needs drew a lot of attention from the primary reason for being there, the wedding of the couple.

The second story occurred when the bride proposed that her uncle, purportedly an opera singer, sing for her wedding. At that time the church where I served had a policy requiring all outside musicians audition before the decision about performing at the wedding was made. Because the uncle was a continent away, this policy was suspended, so that he and I met only thirty minutes before the service. The sound of his voice was so forced and raucous that it was difficult to know what to do. There was no way to disallow his performance since he was already in his tuxedo and the service was about to begin. Would the assembled guests wonder why the minister or parish musician would ever allow such an embarrassing performance? Or should the organist play overloud, "inadvertently" obscuring much of the sound from the uncle's voice? I confess to the latter.

There is no reason to be snobbish. On the other hand, it is wise to be prepared with some policies that help prevent unexpected catastrophes. Just as most clergy would not allow free access to the pulpit by just any individual who asked for it, some consideration of who will make music for the joyful occasion of a wedding must be planned. As is true for the funeral, we don't want worshippers to remember the music either for its excessive showiness or for its poor quality. Our goal is that music is an integral part of the service, adding richness and beauty to this landmark occasion.

Here is the most important criterion in establishing a policy for performers at a wedding (as for a funeral): The musical standards for these occasions should be as close as possible to the standards for the parish's music for a Sunday morning service. Of course, there is a huge variation in musical standards from one parish to another. Often this is because of the resources available. We want the best music *reasonably* available in both circumstances—the wedding service and the Sunday morning worship service. The church is not a concert hall where paying customers expect near-flawless performances, and yet worshippers do come to services with expectations of appropriately performed music. Is it un-Christian to have standards for music at these occasions as we have for a sermon at a regular service or for a meal served to parishioners?

It is usually "the school of hard knocks" that produces policies for that kind of decision making. Policies on the choice of wedding music save having to make fresh judgments for each event. One parish I served, one with very high standards of music performance for regular worship, had a policy that only professional musicians would be engaged, and that only the parish musician would decide who they were to be. In truth, the policy was bent on occasion when family musicians were skilled. Parishes of modest size and resources can seldom have such lofty guidelines. Still, music at the simplest level can be effective, worshipful, and beautiful.

The wedding guidelines need to be fashioned appropriately for each situation, but thinking through them carefully is well worth clergy and musicians' investment of time. A good, fair policy appearing in published guidelines that can be handed to a couple will contribute to a happy, successful, and memorable wedding.

Planning Music for the Wedding

The mother of the bride is not getting married. In many instances the bride's mother exerts a great deal of influence on the shape and content of the service. Clergy will beware the mother who wants (1) to recreate her own wedding or, worse yet, (2) to create the wedding she wanted but was never able to have. Fortunately, most brides' mothers are eager for the couple to plan their own service.

I recall the unusual occasion of getting a call from the mother of the groom, who said, "I am Kitty Vander Schmitz (a fictitious name), and I will be planning the music for my son's wedding. Everyone in the family knows I am a musical snob and that I have to be happy with the music." She proceeded to give me instructions.

A week or two later, the bride called. I said, "Oh yes, I've heard from your future mother-in-law, and she told me that she's planning the music." A long pause followed. Then, "Oh no, she's not."

It was this occasion that caused me to establish the following policy: Nobody but the bride and groom comes for the appointment to plan the music for the wedding— preferably with no parents in tow. Often a parent, intentionally or unwittingly, exerts undue influence, resulting in the couple's having little to say about the music. Ever since encountering the self-proclaimed musical snob, I have required written permission from the bridal couple authorizing someone else, when necessary, to plan the music for a wedding.

Those who have done countless weddings are full of amusing anecdotes, usually of outrageous behavior or things that went wrong. The truth is, however, that most weddings are joyous occasions for everyone concerned, including the clergy and musicians. Weddings can draw people closer to the church, enriching a family's spiritual journey, and offering the couple a spiritual foundation for their life together.

Not only can planning the wedding service be a bonding experience between couple and congregation, but this can also extend to the entire process of preparation for marriage. In one parish where I served, the marriage preparation program was so extensive and so thoroughly implemented that it became the church's greatest implement of evangelism. Many couples, seeing the requirements of that program, chose to go elsewhere. But those who fully participated in the preparation—attending the classes, worshiping on Sunday, taking advantage of the counseling and testing—felt not only that they had been equipped for successful marriage, but also, by the time they completed the program, firmly connected to the parish.

Even though church professionals are inclined to remember the oddities and humorous flukes, most encounters with families at wedding time are entirely positive. Having a published wedding policy—including what music is appropriate—is essential to a smooth experience. In my experience, whenever trouble in wedding planning developed, it was because, as mentioned earlier, a couple made their arrangements before reading the guidelines and before consulting with the clergy and musician. In nearly every instance, when the couple follows the guidelines, and when they include the clergy and musician in planning process, weddings are smooth sailing.

CHAPTER SEVEN

Music and Money

Oh, religion is a fortune, I really do believe,
Oh, religion is a fortune, I really do believe,
Oh, religion is a fortune, I really do believe,
Where Sabbaths have no end.

Why should the parish spend money for a fine music ministry? Other priorities tug at the budget—aspects seen by many as more pressing than a music program. How can we justify spending money on music in light of these? Here's how: Hardly anything touches the lives of so many people—parishioners and community alike—as the music ministry. Music is not an isolated aspect, but instead reaches into multiple areas of church and community life, serving a number of essential functions, described below.

Worship is a high priority for all churches. This is the setting where the largest segment of the congregation gathers regularly— to praise God, to hear Scripture proclaimed, to be fed by Word and Sacrament. It is the place where our identity as individual believers and as a corporate body is focused and rejuvenated. Music sets the tone for worship, fills it with color and energy, actively engages worshipers, and amplifies the seasonal theme, Scripture, and sermon. If the sermon satisfies the left-brain function of worship, music engages the right brain. It touches the soul, raises the spirit, and moves us beyond the ordinary to the numinous. St. Augustine's oft-quoted dictum rings true: "They who sing pray twice."

Christian education occurs throughout an effective music ministry. Not only does this apply to the active participants in the program, but also to the entire worshiping assembly. Even as they sing hymns, worshipers are being instructed in their faith. This is why the hymnal is sometimes called the layperson's book of theology. People remember the words and tunes of hymns, often recalling them, singing bits to themselves, at critical times in their lives. For this reason, the texts to hymns need to be theologically sound and artistically rich. What people sing, they remember.

In addition to worship, participants in the choir experience the most enduring form of Christian education during rehearsals between Sundays. Every text sung at practice offers an opportunity for reflection. Some of the greatest scriptural and poetic passages become the texts of anthems, which both children and adults learn. Indeed, if they rehearse an anthem for several weeks, singers may memorize the words unwittingly, so that they recur in the heart throughout life. This is one way people assimilate their theology—through singing it and reflecting on it.

Liturgy is learned as participants in the music ministry prepare to lead worship musically. Every part of the service needs to be understood so that the musicians fully embody their part in leadership. Choir members are often keen practitioners of liturgy, since their role encourages them to comprehend its function and movement.

Fellowship among members of the parish is enriched when music graces a social event. Music attracts people, binds them together, raises their spirits, and gives them a means to express their joy.

Music touches on all these elements of parish life, not as an isolated feature of the community but a unifying one. It pulls together many disparate components of the parish, strengthening the bonds among them. The parish music ministry is not only for those parishioners who are involved in it as direct participants, but also for the entire community.

For these reasons, investing a substantial portion of the budget in the music ministry can have dramatic and revitalizing results that invigorate the whole parish. Nevertheless, there will be frequent opposition to adequate funding of the music program, and wise clergy will prepare themselves in advance with arguments for its support. Such opposition usually comes from two sources.

When parish finance leaders, staff or volunteer, look for ways to trim the budget, they often look quickly over the figures and target what looks like an excessive amount for music. For reasons that a psychologist could explain better than I, financial people—church treasurers, budget committees, others charged with fiscal responsibility—often seem unsympathetic to funding music.

Perhaps the analytical nature of accounting contrasts with the expressive, emotionally charged nature of music. Indeed, in looking for a good accountant, you want someone who approaches the work with objectivity rather than with feeling. There are blessed exceptions, but the tendency to discount music is apparent in the behavior and value system of many financial folks.

As a young church musician, I questioned a wise minister about our church treasurer's constant attempts to slash the music budget. He answered, "Some people have no poetry in their soul." There may be an element of truth in that. The optimist in me, however, wants to assume that all people have poetic potential. In fact, church music may be most important for those folks who need help finding the poetry in their soul.

This same wise minister was ready every year at budget time to advocate funding for music. Not a musician himself, he had nevertheless witnessed the power of music to animate a congregation, convincing him to become a strong witness to its importance. Each year, and with every change of treasurer, he would firmly say, "No, that is not a place we need to cut funds. Music is the main reason that many people come to our church."

Another source of opposition to music funding comes from people who are advocates for other areas of the church's ministry. I cannot count the number of times I've heard a statement like this: "When you look at the budget item for music, compared with what we spend on children's Christian education, it seems like we don't care much about our children." (Ironically the speaker overlooked the reality that, as is often the case, the vast majority of people in the music ministry were children.) Music is more costly than some other aspects of parish life. Like it or not, this is just the way things are. Music is thus a fragile line item in the parish budget. Compared with other important activities in the parish, music often appears to receive more dollars and is, therefore, vulnerable to cuts.

In that same parish where the advocate for Christian education was concerned about its underfunding, Christian education was, in fact, being done with excellence. The level of funding seemed to provide adequately for materials and resources. But looking at the budget, dollar for dollar, music appeared to be more highly regarded. This is because a dollar-for-dollar comparison is misleading. My automobile costs more than my refrigerator. That does not mean that I value transportation more than food (as anyone who knows me will attest).

As a church musician I greatly value the work and ministry of Christian education, and take every opportunity to affirm those who do it, advocating for more funding. Why these two ministries are often at odds when they are such natural allies is a mystery. It is the infamous "theology of scarcity" that leads us to pit worthwhile ministries against each other to compete for resources. In my experience, contributors are generous when an effective ministry captures their imagination. Amazing results often occur when leaders present their dreams for the ministries to which they believe God is calling people. The miracle of the loaves and fishes is that Jesus moved the disciples from a theology of scarcity to a theology of abundance. If we live this truth, surely our parishes will suddenly discover that all are fed, and with seven baskets of leftovers (Matt 15:37).

What Is Needed to Fund a Music Ministry

A rule of thumb is that the music budget, including salaries, should be about a tenth of the overall parish budget. This can be explained as a tithe of our resources for worship, since nearly every aspect of the music ministry leads to that goal. But what sorts of things are needed?

Salaries

The largest item in a music budget is likely to be the salary (or salaries) of the leader(s) of the music ministry, the Director of Music, Minister of Music, Organist-Choirmaster, or whatever the applicable title. Guidelines available from the website of the American Guild of Organists take into consideration a number of factors: level of education, level of certification (according to AGO examinations), number of hours worked. There is also a link to a website that adjusts salaries to geographical area, urban or rural location, and so forth. A range of salaries for each category in the AGO guidelines is listed, so that years of experience and other factors may be considered. In addition to the AGO, most denominations have professional organizations for church musicians, which also have salary guidelines.

Church musicians are notoriously inept at negotiating financial packages for themselves. For this and for other reasons, it is necessary for the clergyperson who supervises the musician to be an advocate for getting the best salary and benefits (including critical funding for continuing education) possible. Sometimes there is an adversarial role between the musician and the supervisor, who may feel a commitment to the parish to get the best person possible for the least amount of money. Ultimately there is little benefit to saving a few dollars on the musician's salary, and there is potentially a great deal to lose. The highest motivation is justice. Musicians often have trained for many years, and at great deal of expense, to take a job that pays less that many other positions requiring only a couple years of trade school. The reason musicians persist, in the best of circumstances, is their passion for church music, a sense of vocational calling, and their desire to use their musical talents to bless others.

If a church musician is underpaid, several things may happen that adversely affect not only the musicians but also the church: Frequently a very good person leaves a position where he is otherwise happy in order to earn a better livelihood. What is even more unfortunate is that, in many instances, when the parish begins to look for a replacement, it discovers that the salary they have been paying is woefully inadequate, grossly in need of updating, and must be raised in order to attract a person of equal caliber with the one who has just left. If a musician is genuinely called to another place, then she must go, of course, but how unfortunate if it was a matter of not being able to live on the income a parish provides.

A second unhappy scenario occurs when the musician takes on additional employment to supplement an inadequate income. Sometimes this can result in giving short shrift to the duties of parish musician, trying to balance an impossible schedule, and dealing with inevitable calendar conflicts. Very few highly skilled professionals in other fields are called upon to juggle two, three, or four jobs. The quality of ministry is certain to be adversely affected by the fatigue and the fragmentation induced. What we want, regardless the size of the parish, is a musician who has the energy to commit fully to her job, calling upon her creativity to develop a successful program.

Third, a quiet (or sometimes not so quiet) resentment begins to permeate the musician's work. Even if a person tries to maintain a sense of decorum and integrity, such resentment can surface in some unwanted and unhealthy ways. Far better that the salary be a matter of open discussion between the musician and the supervising clergy than that it smolder, sometimes for years, generating tensions, bad relationships, and less than desirable quality of performance.

As seen in the chapter on clergy-musician relations, the exaggerated difference between clergy and musician benefits and salaries—despite education, years of experience, and weekly hours being similar—is a cause for great concern. Even when there is a policy of confidentiality about salaries, this information (or a general sense of it) circulates. Surely our call to justice begins with those who are closest to us. Clergy who find themselves remarking silently that they would never work for the musician's wages might take a serious look at this inequity. Clergy control over this matter varies according to denominational polity, but clergy can always choose to be an ally. How wonderful to hear of those rare instances where parishes pay fair wages, benefits, and give regular adjustments, not only based on cost of living change but also on merit. All these matters are important, whether the musician is part-time or a full-time professional, vocational church musician.

Staff Singers

Nothing causes quite so much difference of opinion as this topic. Customs on paying singers range widely, depending upon denomination, area of the country, size of parish, and tradition. Under the best circumstances, trained singers give support, guidance, and encouragement to volunteers and vastly improve the quality of the choir's music making. I remember the humorous case, many years ago, of a finance committee person who remarked, "I don't know why we need paid professionals in our choir. They are perfectly magnificent!" Little did he know that even given very fine volunteer singers, the professionals were the reason the choir was magnificent.

Having some people who are paid and others who are volunteer all doing the same task can be tricky. When it works, it is because the leadership has laid down very clear principles: The staff singers are there to shepherd and support others, not to assume star status. The attitude of a servant here, as in every aspect of church work, will serve to diffuse any resentment.

Some parishes have a policy that persons hired for the choir must come from outside the congregation, so that there is no internal competition for the positions. When competition does occur, it is certainly not for financial reward. Believe me, the money given to staff singers is never a king's ransom. There must be other motivations.

Often I have observed people who came to the choir primarily as paid singers, but over time became a vital part of the community, participating in aspects of the parish's life other than choir. Never will I forget the parish where all four section leaders felt called to be confirmed at the same time. Nor will I forget the section leader who volunteered to head the parish's hurricane relief ministry.

When wise guidance and grace are present, these people come to see their musical role as a ministry to both choir and parish.

Instrumentalists

Some churches have a tradition of a separate choir director and organist, while others have an organist-choirmaster position. Still others have a pianist in addition to, or instead of, an organist. Others have guitarists or other instrumentalists who play regularly or on occasion. These matters depend upon denomination and parish tradition, taste, and preference.

Besides these regular musicians, parishes have discovered that special instruments for festival services can add an element of celebration, greatly enhancing the occasion. At Christmas and Easter, and other festivals of the church year, including patronal days, musicians performing on brass, percussion, string, or woodwind instruments add an exhilarating element to worship. When parishioners and members of the community learn the pattern of festival music, attendance usually soars on those days.

In one parish where I worked, the rector suggested that rather than have special services or concerts on Sunday afternoons, we might wish to incorporate them into the Sunday morning worship services. After trying this pattern for several years, we discovered to our astonishment that the church was filled to overflowing, so much so that we had to repeat the service twice on Sunday morning to accommodate all the worshipers. In the context of worship, festivals came to be evangelism for the parish, and many people came into the fuller life of the church this way.

These festivals were paid for by parishioners (or members of the community) who wished to honor an anniversary, to remember a loved one, or to mark some other occasion. This meant that no money from the parish budget was required. If such a plan is not followed, then the budget must include money for instrumentalists. Sometimes a contractor (a member of the local orchestra or university music department) will hire the musicians, and this person will recommend how much money is needed.

Instrument Maintenance

If the church has a pipe organ, money must be allocated for its tuning and maintenance. This will vary from one location to another, but a local organ technician can advise the parish on the funds needed. Tunings are needed before major music events, such as Christmas and Easter, and in seasonal weather changes. It is also a good idea to put aside a percentage of the cost of the organ—say 10 percent—for major repairs that may be required every few years.

Pipe organs, though expensive to purchase, are financially sound investments because they last much longer than electronic instruments. When the cost is amortized over the life of the instrument, it amounts to a small amount of money per annum. The best guide to this is the following truism: A ten-year-old electronic organ is ancient; a ten-year-old pipe organ is barely cutting its teeth. In old European churches there are pipe organs still in use that were built in the 1600s or even earlier. Though every organ cannot be expected to last that long, these venerable instruments do point to the durability and sound long-term investment of a pipe organ. All issues of aesthetics aside, money spent on a pipe organ is money well spent.

If your parish is fortunate enough to own a fine pipe organ, it is just good stewardship to make sure that it is properly cared for and maintained. The organ is usually the most expensive piece of equipment on the church property. Setting aside money for its care, and finding a responsible professional to look after it, simply makes good sense.

Pianos

Pianos need to be tuned twice a year, once at the very least, in order to keep them in good condition. Sometimes people have the mistaken notion that tuning is only necessary if your ears are offended by out-of-tune music. While an in-tune piano is more pleasant (and trains developing musicians to hear pitch more accurately), the instrument's longevity is also affected by tuning and maintenance. If a piano goes seriously out of tune after several years' neglect, it is often impossible to tighten the strings enough to bring the instrument into tune without breaking the soundboard.

Churches are notorious for having poor pianos that have been donated by well-meaning families. Sometimes a beautiful cabinet will convince a person that the piano is an excellent instrument, or else the brand name suggests purported value. It is far preferable for a parish to purchase reliable instruments (even used ones) than to fill the building with substandard, donated pianos. Having a technician check an instrument before accepting it is a good policy. If you fear causing offense with this approach, it is probably best to have a general practice not to accept any offers of instruments. More than once I have told a family that there was no space at the church for a piano they wished to give, rather than take a chance of adding another awful instrument to our collection of cast-offs or risking offense.

Harpsichords

The harpsichord is a forerunner of the piano and was in its heyday during the Baroque era. For parishes that have the funds to do so, and whose music programs include lots of early music, owning a harpsichord can add a wonderful flavor to services and concerts.

Handbells

Many churches have handbells that are played by youth (or adults). These are excellent, high-quality musical instruments, and learning to play them can build community among the members of the bell choir, as well as enhance the worship services. Bell choirs often are called upon to play at events in the community as well. Three major manufacturers of handbells are Malmark, Schulmerich, and Whitechapel.

Sheet Music

For each choir or instrumental group, there needs to be an item in the budget for purchasing sheet music. Although music is used again and again, in each season new music needs to be added. In addition to copies for each person, allowance should be made for lost, misplaced, or damaged music. Besides the music for regular

Sunday services, the music director will also need to purchase music for special events and for instrumentalists.

Copyright Licenses

Whenever music is copied, either for musicians or for the worship bulletins, care must be taken to insure that copyright laws are obeyed. It is illegal to copy most music without obtaining written (or Internet) permission. While this used to be a complicated and onerous procedure, it has been made easier in recent years by blanket copyright licenses that cover many publishers. Organizations such as OneLicense.net allow online reporting when churches use the material covered by their company. License fees are modest, based on the size of the worshiping body. A church with twenty-five people in attendance on Sundays, for example, will pay a very small annual fee.

It cannot be overstressed that churches are not exempt from obeying the copyright laws, and, in fact, have an obligation to model ethical practice. Composers of church music make very little money. Most compose from a sense of personal fulfillment or spiritual calling. Publishers base their distribution on sales. If a composition appears not to be selling, publishers declare the title out of print. It is all too common for a church's choral library to be filled with illegal photocopies. (A humorous aside: As a composer, several times, when visiting a parish, I have been honored, to find some of my compositions in a parish's choral library. That's the good news. The bad news is that the music was photocopied.) Many years ago, the nun who was principal of a school where I taught reminded me, "How can we ask composers to write music for the church if their creations are pillaged? Why would publishers continue to print music when they can't sell it because it's being photocopied?" A distinguished composer once told me that the vast majority of his music in libraries throughout the country comprised illegal copies. This not only deprived him of income, but it also sent a false message to his publishers that his music was not selling, inducing them to drop it from their catalog. It is simple and inexpensive to do the right thing regarding copyright laws. Clergy need to make sure their churches budget the money for it.

There are, of course, other items that might be included in a music budget. Clergy, when they are fortunate enough to have seasoned musicians develop and implement a music budget, may have less responsibility and concern about it. For small congregations, however, the clergy may indeed be the one to develop the music budget. Even in large parishes, it is helpful when the clergy understand elements in the cost of running an excellent music ministry.

CHAPTER EIGHT

Hiring a Musician

Little David, play on your harp,
Hallelu, hallelu,
Little David, play on your harp,
Hallelu.

Why do I, as clergy, with a million things to do already, need to care about hiring a musician? Isn't there someone else, or some committee, that could handle this without my help? No. Your hands-on involvement is needed in such an important task.

The effectiveness of the music ministry in your church will be largely dependent upon leadership. Music programs are no different from parishes in that regard. Having hired a number of musicians and acted as search consultant to churches looking for an ideal candidate to fit their ideas and programs, I have learned some of the challenges (and some of the errors) that can occur in musician searches, as indeed in clergy searches. There is never a guarantee of success, of course, even if you approach the task methodically, diligently, and with the guidance of the Holy Spirit. But that approach will avoid some of the roadblocks and miseries, easily surpassing a haphazard, random search.

This chapter offers very detailed information on the process of hiring a church musician. There are some guidelines that pertain to any congregation, followed by a section especially for small parishes—both urban and rural—whose search process makes different demands.

Preparing for a Search

Clergy will know the wisdom of enlisting the assistance of music program "stakeholders" when undertaking a musician search. The people who have a history with the parish's music ministry and who have demonstrated a deep concern for it are your essential constituency. If you are new to the parish and not sure who they are, it is important to ask around. Besides their wisdom and guidance, you also need these stakeholders as advocates and cheerleaders on behalf of the new musician when she arrives. Even on the off chance that you alone happen to select the perfect candidate, the new leader may have an impossible task ahead if he is confronted with a phalanx of opposition from those who felt they had no voice in his selection process.

Small committees are more fleet of foot than large ones, but you also need representatives from several constituencies: the choir(s), making sure you include parents of children's choirs and representatives from the teenage choirs; some members of the congregation who don't sing in a choir; members of the vestry, session, or church board; and a person involved in the finances of the parish. No paid staff member who will be working under the new leader's supervision should be included. If your parish has the resources, it is economically wise to hire a consultant, especially in (but not limited to) those situations where the person will be a full-time staff person. Locating a consultant is not difficult. You might want to begin by asking trusted clergy, perhaps especially any who have recently conducted a successful search. In light of the ease of electronic communication, the consultant need not even be in your geographical area.

Criteria

The search committee (and consultant, if there is one) will help you compile a list of criteria that you consider essential for a successful music ministry. There are two common errors you will hope to avoid. One, people may find it easier to identify what they wish to change than what it is they want to keep; two, the list of criteria can easily grow so long that no person on earth could possibly fulfill it all. (Both these mistakes occur regularly in clergy searches, too.)

The first error, focusing only on change, occurs because people sometimes take all that is going well for granted, assuming that these are givens that will always remain. Not so. I have seen many parishes that are so concentrated on the many changes they desire that they lose the very things most precious to them about their parish with the selection of the new leader. As tempting as it is to do otherwise, try to begin the discussion of criteria with the things presently valued in the existing music program, and then prioritize them.

The second error, compiling a humanly impossible list, may satisfy the committee, particularly if everyone at the table gets to add her favorite criterion. But it will leave potential candidates unfocused on what you seek, or else will overwhelm them and drive them away.

The committee's discussion will produce a job description. When compiling the list, suggestions may be all over the map. Have a good writer prepare the job description, going from general goals to specific duties. Create an opening paragraph that describes in a few words what your committee sees as the mission of this particular church's music ministry. Once the general tenor of this statement has been decided, assign it to a clear wordsmith. Nothing is more frustrating than wording by committee.

Once you compile the list of desired traits and characteristics and have prioritized it, trim, trim, trim. It should fit on a half sheet of paper. Saying too much will dilute the impact of your job description. Besides, publications that advertise the position (see below) will not accept long advertisements. Even if someone's favorite item must be sacrificed, the process will be better served by brevity.

Advertising

Whether the position is only a few hours a week or full-time, it pays to use print and Internet advertising. There are three primary publications to consider, and all three will probably cost you no money. The first is the *American Organist*, the monthly magazine of the American Guild of Organists. Even if the person you are seeking is primarily a conductor rather than an organist, this journal will be helpful. There are, however, three frustrations that people have experienced using the *American Organist*: First, the lead time required is longer than one wishes, so that the ad may not appear until you are well into your search. Second, the number of responses may overwhelm you, particularly if the position is full-time. Third, the applicants may not be from your denomination, if that matters to you. Still, this is a very attractive avenue for recruiting a large pool of applicants from which to make an eventual short list of candidates.

The second publication is *The Choral Journal*, which is the monthly magazine of the American Choral Directors Association. This will be more helpful if you are particularly interested in the talents of a choral director and vocal leadership in worship rather than a leader who is a combination organist-director.

The third publication is the journal of the professional organization for church musicians in your denomination. Nearly all denominations have such an organization and newsletter or journal, often also having a placement service. Registering with the placement service will allow you access to church musicians who are actively seeking positions. The placement officer, if there is one, may also agree to talk with you directly. All these publications are likely to have online advertising as well.

When Applications Are Received

It is preferable to copy the important parts of the applicants' submissions, distributing them to all committee members, rather than dividing the packets among the committee. If you choose the latter approach, you may miss a sterling candidate that any one particular committee member didn't like. When committee members read the applications, it will be helpful to have the job description at hand. Otherwise, it is easy to become distracted by irrelevant data. Committee members should be encouraged to look not only for matches, but also for uniqueness. There may be something unexpected about a candidate that makes her jump to the top of your list. Being open to surprises is important: Sometimes the most unlikely candidate may be your new leader.

I find it best to have committee members individually sort the applications in order of their preference, and then bring their results to the committee meeting. This will avoid the strong-voiced members of the committee (including certain clergy) from holding sway over the process. It is far more enlightening to compare various individual opinions than to arrive initially at a group consensus, which may well be the opinion of only the most outspoken.

It is very important to communicate with all applicants in a thoughtful and timely manner. Churches have a dismal track record on this. I am still waiting to hear from a church where I interviewed in person twenty years ago, and I am just about ready to give up thinking they will ever hire me! Many search committees choose to hold all their applications until the search is completed. This is usually unnecessary and cruel. The committee will read a certain number of letters from applicants that are instantly seen as inappropriate for the position. It is only gracious to send them a prompt letter, thanking them for their interest, saying that many applications were received from highly qualified candidates, and unfortunately the search committee determined their qualifications as not matching the criteria set by the committee. Then wish them the very best in their search for a position. This letter should be polite, short, and avoid details about the process. It can be a form letter and does not need to contain personalized references to the candidate other than her name.

The remaining candidates should also be informed rapidly. Sometimes musicians will have applied to more than one place. Not communicating with them can mean losing them. Some years ago I applied for a position with a church from which I heard nothing for months. After I had relocated to another parish, I received a panicked phone call from the first church, saying that I was their choice and would I please consider coming for an interview. I asked them what they would think of me if I agreed to interview with them after having been in a new job for five weeks. They decided to pursue other candidates.

Your list at this point, provided you have received an adequate number of applications, should probably number three to five. When you write to those on your short list, it is inappropriate to indicate the number of candidates. If you have determined the details of the process at this point, you might state the time line of the decision. For example, "We hope to interview candidates in person during March and reach a decision by mid-April." Again, this is a courtesy to people who are concerned about the length of the process, and it might assist the decision of a candidate who is being considered by more than one parish. Many times I have known candidates who were playing roulette with several applications. "If I say 'no' to this parish in which I'm moderately interested, I still might not get an offer later from the one I strongly want," and so forth. Mainly, don't hesitate to stay in communication. E-mail is perfectly acceptable, as long as you are assured of its being received by getting a response. We all know of important e-mails that never went through.

References

Your advertisement will, of course, have requested references (usually three) for the candidates. A wise candidate will request letters from prominent people of his or her acquaintance: professors, supervisors, and professional colleagues in church music. I have never understood one curious omission—references from parishioners who have worked closely under the musician's leadership. Sometimes these people know the church musician in a working environment better than her clergy supervisor.

Two glaring errors commonly occur with regard to references: First, the candidate gives a list of people to be contacted, but the search committee or clergy never bother to approach the referee. Countless times I have agreed to serve as a referee for someone about whom I never received a call, letter, or e-mail. It clearly doesn't make sense to proceed without a social and professional history of the candidate from those who know him or her best.

The second common error is considering only the references that a person gives you. All of us, when applying for a job, submit only the names of referees who are card-carrying members of our fan club. While this is flattering, and, depending upon the personality of the referee, may even give some pertinent information about the applicant, it seldom reveals any significant flaws. Once the application materials are reviewed, any well-connected clergy, church musician, or consultant will immediately think of people to contact other than those listed as referees. Especially if the person contacting the referee has a professional connection with that person, you may discover aspects of the candidate—good or bad—that haven't been evident in any of the conventional ways.

There are two times in a long career that I have made drastic mistakes when hiring a musician. Neither person lasted very long. In retrospect (always crystal clear), these might have been easily avoided had I checked the candidate's background with people who were in the position to observe her or his behavior and performance, but whose names were not on the referee list. The undesirable behavior that rendered the new employee unacceptable was clearly evident in his work history, only we discovered it too late. One caveat to this approach is that for legal reasons, employers are sometimes allowed to reveal only the dates of a person's tenure and nothing more; of course, you will need to follow the law in your own jurisdiction. Nevertheless, checking with referees—those submitted, as well as others—is a critically important aspect of your search process.

Site Visits to Candidates

If your resources permit, sending a couple of committee members to visit candidates in their current positions will meet a number of needs. First of all, the best forecaster of success is a great track record. Even if a person is in a more modest situation than yours, even if it is remarkably different—another denomination, for example—you can still get an idea of how he functions where he is. Visiting a candidate in her own setting may also help to preserve her anonymity. It is easier for committee members to go to her than for her to ask off a Sunday with vague explanations. Maintaining the confidence of applicants is paramount. The world of church music is a small circle, and information travels quickly. A candidate does not want her superior to discover she has applied for another position until the time is right, and then she wants the employer to hear it directly, not through the grapevine.

Before representatives of the search committee travel to observe candidates on their own turf, the committee should develop a template of questions and procedures that will be followed with each candidate. This will allow for an easier comparison later.

If the candidate agrees, the representatives might wish to speak with one or two people in her current position. Normally this will not include the musician's supervising clergy, unless they have a relationship that makes this possible. When she has concerns about confidentiality, she may ask that you not speak with anyone while visiting. This is a reasonable request.

The entire committee will be eager to hear the reports from representatives who have made site visits to the candidates. This process should further reduce the number of candidates to two or three. It could possibly even lead to one shining candidate.

Site Visits from the Candidates

Bringing the candidate to visit your parish is important enough to warrant dealing with the difficulties involved. Some churches wisely arrange that a candidate not visit on Sunday, lest they inadvertently come to involve the entire parish in the decision process. One clergyman told me that he feared parishioners' falling in love with a candidate who did not work out. This argues for limiting direct contact with the candidate to those involved in the search process. The other difficulty of a Sunday visit is that the candidate must explain why he is missing church in his current position, and perhaps he is not ready to do that.

The candidate's visit needs to include a number of stops. Obviously the clergy supervisor needs to meet with the candidate privately. Most musicians (and clergy) feel that no matter what else seems right, if this relationship doesn't work, the match will never be satisfactory. Other key staff members should meet with the candidate, privately if possible. Half-hour meetings might be sufficient, and often a seasoned staff member, lay or ordained, will pick up something important.

The entire committee should meet with the candidate in a social setting. If the first face-to-face meeting is an interview, it can be intimidating and off-putting. Often a social situation gives a better impression than an interview for the way a candidate may work with and relate to people. If the candidate is an introvert, that should be taken into account when assessing her behavior in a large group. Even extreme introverts make excellent leaders and shouldn't be overlooked. You don't want to utterly exhaust the candidate; realize that he is in a strange environment, may be weary from travel, and must go through all steps of the routine you establish—as opposed to your part, consisting of only one or two steps. Still, the more stations in the visit, the more observers you have, the better the chance for a mutually agreeable decision. (Keep in mind that the interview process involves discernment on both sides.)

The Audition—Organ

If the person is an organist, she needs to play for the entire committee. When there is no informed listener on the committee, an outside consultant who knows organ playing needs to be included. I have known many seasoned clergy, however—even those not particularly trained in music—who have learned over the years to adjudicate organists skillfully. In addition to performing organ literature (the kind of music that usually appears at preludes and postludes, or opening and closing voluntaries), the organist needs to improvise (if that skill is used in your services), accompany, and play hymns. It amazes me that parishes often hear only organ literature at an audition, when, in fact, such prepared compositions constitute a very small portion of an organist's duties. Far more important for the worship service is the musician's ability to lead the congregational singing by the way he or she plays hymns and service music (those regularly recurring items such as the Sanctus or the Doxology).

Playing hymns is an art, one unfortunately dismissed in some music schools. Certain professors of organ, for reasons I will never understand, assume that they are training concert artists, and deny the importance of hymn playing. The fact is that only a handful of organists in the world subsist on their income from concertizing. Most organists play for churches and, therefore, congregational singing. I have heard of organ professors who say, "What's to playing a hymn? You just open up the hymnal and play the notes on the page." Spoken like an organist who doesn't understand hymn singing . . .

The major distinguishing characteristic of an organist who knows how to play hymns is leadership. This organist is not just playing notes, but is conscious of leading the congregation in singing, which has multiple ramifications for how the instrument is played. For example, is the congregation clear when to begin singing, or confused—both at the outset of the hymn after the introduction, and from one verse to the next? Is the registration (the selection of sounds on the organ) appropriate? Does the organist vary the registration from one stanza of the hymn to the next, or even within a given stanza? Does the registration reflect the text? (For example, if we are singing "Drop thy still dews of quietness," the organ should not be full blast.) Does the tempo (speed) take the acoustics of the room into consideration? (A live, reverberant space may call for a slower pace than a dry, acoustically dead space.) Does the organist phrase the music according to the text, breaking or sustaining where the text seems to indicate? Does the organist play so loudly as to obliterate the congregation's effort to sing, or does he or she support and encourage them?

If the organist will also be the choir director, she needs to play and conduct simultaneously as part of the audition. (See below for choral audition.)

Ample practice time on a strange instrument must be allowed for the candidate, and the interview schedule should not be so tightly packed as to preclude this opportunity. Every organ is different, not at all like moving from one piano to another. Though pianos differ, too, organs can be extremely distinct. Even a highly skilled organist will not know immediately how to deal with an unfamiliar instrument until familiarizing herself with it. If the organ in your church has peculiar quirks, it is only fair to have someone who knows the instrument explain them to the candidate. Even if this is done, and even if adequate practice time happens, allow for some bobbles when this is the first time she has ever played this instrument.

After the interview, everyone on the committee should be heard when assessing the organist. Even if a committee member insists she knows nothing about organs, she probably knows a good deal more than she thinks about organ playing after a lifetime of attending church. Not commanding the technical vocabulary to describe a response doesn't mean her observation isn't valid. I once had a clergy colleague who claimed to know nothing about music but his remarks about the previous Sunday's music were as accurate and appropriate as any *New York Times* music critic.

The Audition—Choral Directing

Some parishes have an organist-choirmaster, responsible for both jobs. Others have a tradition of separate people for these two jobs. Still others move occasionally from one arrangement to the other. Sometimes an organist has little training in dealing with choral groups. All her training and experience may have been at the keyboard, in which case she cannot be expected to have equal expertise in both areas. Often I have found that people who do both are an organist-choirmaster with a capital "O," or one with a capital "C"—that is, he has both skills, but excels in one and has learned to accommodate the other. That having been said, there are a number of professional church musicians who are equally adept, and even superb, at both organ playing and choral directing.

The choral audition can be thirty to forty-five minutes and should include choral literature both familiar and unfamiliar to the choir. In prearrangement, the candidate should be sent a couple of anthems that the choir knows well, where the notes are already in place, allowing him to demonstrate his ability to polish and refine the singing. In this case he will work on diction (pronunciation, particularly consonants), balance (hearing the different sections of the choir with none dominating the other unless called for by the music), blend (singing so that individual voices don't stand out but meld together), style (the character of the piece in terms of the performance practice of the historic period), dynamics (loudness and softness of various sections of the music), tone (the beauty of sound the singers produce), vowels (the purity of vowel sounds and consistency among the singers in singing one exact sound), and the like. If singing in languages other than English is expected in your parish, one of the anthems might be in another language.

The candidate will also bring at least one anthem that she knows but that the choir does not. She will teach the choir this new composition, so that the choir and the committee members can observe her ability to communicate, to listen and respond, and to convey to the choir the spirit of the music and the text. These are markedly different skills than those described above. Though she may be expected to cover some aspects detailed above, the teaching process (especially when the choir is mostly volunteer musicians) will concentrate on learning new notes and words.

The choral audition puts the candidate on the spot in an entirely different way than the organ audition. Even though the committee might wish to take the nerves of the candidate into consideration, it is still possible to get a sense of whether a person is capable of dealing with choral groups. A sense of humor is always a sign that a conductor is used to working with people, since it is virtually impossible to lead without one. With a first-class conductor, there is a magic spark evident in her work with a choir—a sense of urgency and energy that generates excitement and passion.

Audition—Children

If the candidate is expected to work with children, the interview-audition process should definitely include a rehearsal session with kids. The musical skills of working with adults and children are similar in many ways, but the social aspects—classroom management, ability to relate intergenerationally, skill at communicating clearly and without condescension—are different. Like the rehearsal with adults, there should be music that is both familiar to the children and new music for the candidate to teach them.

It is unwise to have a large group of adults observing the children. One expert in children's choirs whom I knew felt so strongly about this that she would assign any adults in the room a part to sing. Depending on the children's age, the physical arrangement of the room, and the familiarity of the adults, children being watched may not be themselves, and may not participate at all. It is also trickier for a strange conductor to work with children than adults, because children like to get to know someone before they open up. This is a characteristic we want them to have, for reasons of safety, but it must be taken into account in judging how the candidate fares in that part of the interview.

If the candidate has come from out of town, it is thoughtful to book them into a hotel rather than have them stay with a parish family. When one is being scrutinized during interviews, it is nice to have some time to oneself rather than feeling the obligation to relate to strangers in the evening. Assigning only one person to accompany the candidate from one place to the other during the process can make her feel more comfortable than if a new person meets her at every turn.

After the Interview–Audition

The committee should meet as soon as possible after each candidate visit. When the final candidate has departed, the committee should arrange to come to a conclusion quickly. Nothing is more cruel than leaving the candidates (particularly the first one to visit) hanging indefinitely without any word. While this is only one aspect of your parish's communal life, keep in mind that it affects the candidate's entire existence. If you absolutely cannot reach an immediate decision, it is only fair to contact the candidates with a progress report. "We met on Wednesday night and felt that we needed more time. We'd like to meet again on Sunday. Are you willing to wait until then for us to reach a decision?" After all, she is entirely within her rights to say no, or, not hearing from you, to decide not to be considered further. If you are interested (or even if you're not), it is only charitable to stay in touch as frequently as possible. I have known candidates who decided, on the basis of how they were treated during the search process, to remove themselves from consideration. The standard of Christian behavior remains "do unto others as you would have them do unto you" (Luke 6:31).

The confidential nature of negotiation is between two parties, the candidate and the parish, and both parties need to consider the other in deciding when to break the confidentiality. More than once I have seen a parish announce its decision before the candidate had had ample opportunity to communicate with key people (the most important being her current boss).

Sometimes the best-laid plans go awry. Here is an unlikely tale. I knew a clergyperson from the Southwest who was interviewing for a position in New England. The committee wanted to hear him preach, so rather than chance word of his candidacy spreading prematurely, they moved the site of his trial sermon to a nearby parish. The very next Sunday a woman from the trial sermon parish in New England showed up at the candidate's home church in Albuquerque and said to someone, "You know, it's the strangest thing, but there was a priest from your parish preaching in my church in Vermont last Sunday." Alas, these things will happen, but we must do our best to protect all parties and strive to maintain confidentiality.

After the decision is made, an offer tendered and accepted, and the appropriate contract (or letter of agreement) signed, the remaining candidates should be informed immediately. It is good if the person who shepherded a finalist through the process can deliver a personal message to him. It is not necessary to give many details, nor is it helpful to explain why he didn't get the position. If the winning candidate has no further needs for confidentiality, it is perfectly acceptable to tell the other candidates who has been chosen. In many cases the candidates will all know each other, and they may already be aware of their competition. It is good to thank them heartily for applying for the position and allow them to deal with their own disappointment. As badly as you may feel for them and no matter how strong your pastoral instincts, you are not the best person to help.

Transitions

A search committee often becomes a transition committee. Although the job seems over for the committee members, the changes are just beginning, especially for the new musician. She will need assistance with finding housing, if coming from a distance, finding schools for any children, locating employment for a spouse, learning the area, if it is new, and, most of all, getting to know the people in the parish. Since the search committee and clergy are probably the only people she knows, it is only fair to keep those connections alive and let them help the new employee get adjusted. Sometimes, if left on her own, she will be offered "help" by needy people in the parish who are really require help themselves. Far better that the search committee add a few more weeks to their commitment, and see that the new musician has as graceful a transition as possible.

Small Congregations

Much of what appears above will be directly applicable to a small church looking for a part-time musician. Some aspects, however, require different consideration. Although people do relocate for part-time positions, that is unusual. One of the few times this works is when part-time positions "yoke" with one another. In other words, a church and a school, each of which has a part-time position, agree to look together for one person. Another occasion when a part-time job might attract someone from out of area is when the spouse is taking a new job in your area. Otherwise, part-time candidates usually come from the same area.

It is still a good idea to advertise in the ways suggested above, particularly if your church is in an urban area. In a dense population it is very likely that there are people available for your parish's part-time job with whom you have no direct or indirect connection. Otherwise, you would not find each other.

In a small town or rural area, however, different tactics are needed to find a parish musician. It may be productive to advertise in local newspapers. In many cases, a clergyperson may need to develop a church musician from whatever musician is available. In other places in this book, there are methods and organizations to help with this process.

There are specific places to look for people who might be willing to assist you with your parish music. Public school teachers often take church positions. Even if the ones you contact aren't interested, they may know others who are. Don't rule out retired teachers. They may want to take on a job that requires only a few hours a week.

Piano teachers may be another good source of potential church musicians, even if they have never been church musicians. Still another pool for candidates are people in other vocations who have expertise in music. I know of a church musician who worked in the office of a large lumber company, and another church musician who is an attorney. In each case, the quality of their work could not have been higher had each been a full-time, vocational church musician.

The disadvantage of less populated areas is fewer candidates, but the advantage is that most people know each other. Following even the most unlikely lead may take you directly to the one that works, and one is all you need. The other advantage in a less populated area is that it is usually easier to get from one place to another, so people may not be averse to traveling longer distances. Your inquiries may need to cover a large geographical area. I have known church musicians who drove several hours to their destination. If the connection is a happy one, if the pay worthwhile, the job rewarding, and the vocational call strong enough, there can be a long and fruitful association.

Conclusion

"A good wife who can find? Her value is more than fine gems." The writer of Proverbs 31:10 obviously never hired a musician for the temple, or the passage might've read, "A good temple musician who can find? Her value is more than fine gems." There are far more good wives (and husbands) than church musicians. If it seems impossible to find the right musician for your parish and you become discouraged in the process, just look around and you will notice that there are churches that manage to find excellent musicians. It happens regularly.

Some people are alarmed at the diminishing supply of church musicians, particularly organists, but nothing will turn that around more quickly than the availability of good jobs—jobs where the church musician is given fair wages and benefits, provided the resources needed, and, most of all, treated with kindness, respect, and consideration. Come to think of it, this is not much different from what clergy want.

Where There Is a Vision, the People Flourish

I got a harp, you got a harp,
All o' God's chillen got a harp,
When I get to heab'n I'm goin' to take up my harp,
I'm goin' to play all ovah God's heab'n, heab'n, heab'n.
Ev'ybody talkin' 'bout heab'n ain't goin' there, heab'n, heab'n.
I'm goin' to play all ovah God's heab'n.

Most priests and pastors are already convinced of the benefits of a fine music program in their parish because they have seen the effects of great music. Perhaps they were fortunate enough to belong to such a parish, or they have worked in one in the past, or at least they have observed one from afar.

If you have not been blessed with the firsthand experience of a strong music ministry, locate one near you. Get to know the clergy there, as well as the musician who leads the program. Perhaps you can take a few days to observe the program in action. Even professional church musicians with years of experience find it enlightening to spend time observing an excellent music ministry, studying, asking questions, testing ideas, looking for new approaches that work.

If you have never experienced the impact of great church music, and if it's important to you, finding the time and the situation to make that happen might change your ministry. It's worth a try.

You will find that most churches with a powerful music ministry have a story to tell, one that they are eager to share. Chances are that such a program has not always existed in that parish, and they can tell you how they got to the point where they are.

Two short stories will illustrate examples of such parishes. The first is a large, dynamic parish with many choirs, handbell choirs, small ensembles (performing groups), and a concert series. This was not always the case. There was one clergyperson who believed in the transformative power of music and who shepherded the parish through the process that led them to this complex, successful program.

When he arrived as rector of this parish, there was one music group, a small professional choir of eight voices. His request that the part-time music director recruit parishioners for the choir was met with refusal, eventually resulting in the music director's dismissal. A new organist-choirmaster was located, and the position was yoked with a teaching position at a local parochial school. This afforded the musician a full-time income and made it possible for him to relocate.

Eventually, as the church expanded and the music program grew, the leadership made the music director's position full-time. The parish continued the policy of eight staff singers, but now their job was to support the parish choir, which after a few years numbered sixty-five voices. Children's choirs were begun and had an amazing impact, not just on the children, but also on the entire parish. After years of building, this program included twelve music groups, including people from preschool through retirement age, with over two hundred participating.

The second story is about a small parish. They were able to hire a part-time graduate student to play the organ and to direct a modest choir. The young man was incredibly dynamic, working much harder than his job called for. The music ministry grew in quality and in number of participants. As the organist-choirmaster approached completion of his graduate degree, a sense of panic set in among members of the church. What would they do once this young man had moved on to a full-time job? Would the music program return to its former state? Now that a music ministry of quality had transformed worshipers, how would they adjust to losing it?

The priest determined that something needed to be done, and that she needed to act quickly before this era of enriched music became a thing of the past. She gathered interested parishioners to devise a strategy that led eventually to offering the musician a full-time job upon graduation. He was a talented musician who well might get other offers, but they hoped and prayed that he would choose to stay with them. In fact, that's exactly what happened. The priest admits that she was scared, because she wasn't at all sure how a small parish with its limited income would pay for the music program. On the other hand, she knew that the parish simply couldn't do without it, once great music had become part of their identity. She also knew that starting a music ministry with little money to pay for it was frightening; at the same time, she was convinced that a life of faith involves risk.

As if hiring this new musician was not challenging enough, the priest had come to realize that their small, inexpensive organ was not adequate and needed to be replaced. Not only did it not meet the parish's needs, but also it was not the kind of instrument that would attract a fine musician. Shortly after taking the leap of faith to offer this young man a full-time job, they entered into a program of raising the money to build a new pipe organ. Only a couple years have passed, but already the music ministry is a major aspect of this small congregation's life. It attracts new members and encourages current members to stay. Having heard their choir, I can see why these parishioners feel so strongly about their music ministry. The energy, enthusiasm, and enrichment it brings to worship, indeed, to the entire life of the parish, speak volumes to the power of music in a congregation.

None of this could happen, of course, without extraordinary leadership. But it began as a vision. It started because a clergyperson was convinced that the parish had a new dimension that it could not lose. The question "Can we afford to do this?" led to the more urgent question, "Can we afford *not* to do this?"

Congregations look to their clergy for vision. There is a passage from Proverbs that says, "Where there is no vision, the people perish" (Prov 29:18). Some years ago I came to understand this Scripture best with an opposite reading. With apologies to the Hebrew Scripture, I read this verse as follows: "Where there is a vision, the people flourish."

A great music ministry begins with vision. With intentional planning, location of outstanding leadership, provision of the necessary resources, and, above all, with prayer and the guidance of God's Spirit, the vision can materialize. The fruits of such a ministry are seen primarily in the lives of people. There is little that changes the life of a congregation like great music. People are transformed and blessed, the community is given a new sense of vitality, and, most of all, the worship of God assumes new power and beauty. Amen.

Notes

Chapter One

1. Superscriptions: At the head of each chapter in this book is a quote from a Negro spiritual. In my opinion, these songs are the finest folk music ever created in the United States. What's more important, though, is that they mine profound spiritual truths in simple, elegant language.

2. Fyodor Dostoevsky, *The Idiot*, trans. Constance Garnett (New York: Bantam, 1981), 370.

3. Alexandr Solzhenitsyn, lecture to the Swedish Academy, reprinted in *Nobel Lectures, Literature 1968–1980*, ed. Sture Allén (Singapore: World Scientific Publishing Co., 1993), 35.

4. Erik Routley, *The Church and Music: An Enquiry into the History, the Nature, and the Scope of Christian Judgment on Music* (London: Gerald Duckworth and Co., 1950), 161. Quoted in Paul Westermeyer, *Te Deum: The Church and Music* (Minneapolis: Fortress Press, 1998), 214.

5. Betty Edwards, *Drawing on the Right Side of the Brain* (New York: Jeremy P. Tarcher, 1989), xi.

6. Oliver Sachs, *Musicophilia* (New York: Alfred A. Knopf, 2007).

7. Ibid., 165–67.

8. See, for example, these books on reading music: Earl Henry, *Sight Singing* (Upper Saddle River, N.J.: Prentice Hall, 1997); Paul Schmeling, *Berklee Music Theory* (Boston: Berklee Press, 2005); Robert W. Ottman and Frank D. Mainous, *Rudiments of Music* (Upper Saddle River, N.J.: Prentice Hall, 1995).

9. E-mail correspondence with Wycliffe missionary linguist Judith Schram, July and August 2008.

10. E-mail correspondence with Judith Schram, November 2007.

11. Randy Bishop, "How a Brazilian Tribe Learned to Sing to God," *Christianity Today International / Today's Christian* (formerly *Christian Reader*) 36, no. 4 (July/August 1998): 37.

12. Jack and Jo Popjes, "Music to Their Ears," *Mission Frontiers: The Bulletin of the U.S. Center for World Mission* 8 (May–August 1996): 15.

13. Ibid.

14. Ibid.

15. Donald P. Hustad in a class lecture, Southern Seminary, Louisville, Kentucky, School of Church Music, October 1975.

Chapter Two

1. Alec Wyton, "The Function of Music in Corporate Worship," *The Journal of Church Music* (December 1987), 9.

2. The Leadership Program for Musicians offers clergy and musicians an extensive curriculum in the practice of church music. See their website www.lpm-online.org for information on this highly effective program of study.

3. Wyton was an Anglican (Episcopalian). In certain other U.S. denominations, this concept would not have appeared so radical.

4. The setting we were singing was *Love bade me welcome* by David Hurd (Pittsburgh: Selah Publishing Co.). The same text appears in Ralph Vaughan Williams' *Five Mystical Songs* (Boston: ECS Publishing Co.).

5. Love bade me welcome, yet my soul drew back,
    Guilty of dust and sin.
    But quick-ey'd Love, observing me grow slack
    From my first entrance in,
    Drew nearer to me, sweetly questioning
    If I lack'd anything.

    "A guest," I answer'd, "worthy to be here";
    Love said, "You shall be he."
    "I, the unkind, the ungrateful? ah my dear,
    I cannot look on thee."
    Love took my hand and smiling did reply,
    "Who made the eyes but I?"

    "Truth, Lord, but I have marr'd them; let my shame
    Go where it doth deserve."
    "And know you not," says Love, "who bore the blame?"
    "My dear, then I will serve."

"You must sit down," says Love, "and taste my meat."
So I did sit and eat.
—George Herbert, 1593–1633
The Oxford Book of English Verse 1250–1900, ed. A.T. Quiller-Couch (Oxford: Clarendon, 1906). 295.

6. *The Hymnal 1982*, no. 667.

Chapter Three

1. Robert Burns, "To a Louse," in *The Penguin Book of Scottish Verse*, ed. Robert Crawford and Mick Imlah (London: Penguin Books, 2000), 286.

2. Tennessee Williams, *A Streetcar Named Desire* (New York: New Directions Books, 1947), 165.

3. Paul Westermeyer, *Te Deum: The Church and Music* (Minneapolis: Fortress Press, 1998), 3.

Chapter Four

1. Jerome P. Reiter, *AAM Millenium Survey* (Little Rock, Ark.: Association of Anglican Musicians, 2001), http://anglicanmusicians.org/id9.html

2. H. Wiley Hitchcock, *Music in the United States: A Historical Introduction* (Upper Saddle River, N.J.: Prentice Hall, 1969 [revised, 2000]), 55–56

3. Carol Doran, "Popular Religious Song," in *The Hymnal 1982 Companion* Volume I, ed. Raymond F. Glover (New York: Church Publishing, 1995), 13–28.

4. Edward Schillibeeckx, *Jesus: an Experiment in Christology* (New York: Seabury, 1979), 577.

5. E-mail correspondence with Betty Carr Pulkingham, August 27, 2008.

6. Conversations with Betty Carr Pulkingham that took place over a number of years between 1990 and 2008.

7. Words by Joe Young and Sam M. Lewis, music by Walter Donaldson (New York: Waterson, Berlin & Snyder Co., Music Publishing, 1919).

8. Thomas Cahill, *How the Irish Saved Civilization* (New York: Nan A. Talese/Doubleday, 1995).

9. Paul Westermeyer, *Te Deum: The Church and Music* (Minneapolis: Augsburg, 1998), 278.

10. Michael Hawn, ed., *Halle Halle: We Sing the World Around* (Dallas: Choristers Guild), 1999.

11. *Global Praise*, vols. I, II, and III (New York: General Board of Global Ministries, 1996, 2000, 2004).

12. Interviews and observations made by the author from a sabbatical trip to the Taizé Community in October 1992.

13. From the Iona website www.iona.org.uk.

14. Ibid.

15. Conversations with Betty Carr Pulkingham that took place over a number of years between 1990 and 2008.

Chapter Five

1. Marti Rideout, teaching in the Leadership Program for Musicians, Virginia Theological Seminary, Alexandria, Virginia, July 1995.

2. *Sicut cervus* on the text of Psalm 42, "As the deer longs for cooling streams . . ."

3. The Royal School of Church Music website is http://www.rscm.com/about_us/index.php.

4. John Bertalot, *Teaching Adults to Sight-Sing* (Buxhall, U.K.: Kevin Mayhew Publications, 2004), 40.

5. For the particulars of this curriculum (which is also intended for adults), see the series "Voice for Life," Leah Perona-Wright, ed. (Salisbury, U.K.: Royal School of Church Music, 2004) or see the website http://www.rscmamerica.org/VFL-Awards.htm. An additional resource is "The Voice for Life Chorister's Companion," a pocket-sized, two-hundred-page book with information for the young chorister about singing, reading music, organs, the Church and its liturgy, ed. Tim Ruffer (Salisbury, U.K.: Royal School of Church Music, 2009).

Bibliography

Books

Bertalot, John. *Teaching Adults to Sight-Sing*. Buxhall, U.K.: Kevin Mayhew Publications, 2004.

Burns, Robert. "To a Louse," in *The Penguin Book of Scottish Verse*. Robert Crawford and Mick Imlah, eds. London: Penguin Books, 2000, 286.

Cahill, Thomas. *How the Irish Saved Civilization*. New York: Nan A. Talese/Doubleday, 1995.

Doran, Carol. "Popular Religious Song," in *The Hymnal 1982 Companion* Volume I. Edited by Raymond F. Glover. New York: Church Publishing, 1995.

Dostoevsky, Fyodor. *The Idiot*. Constance Garnett, trans. New York: Bantam, 1981.

Edwards, Betty. *Drawing on the Right Side of the Brain*. New York: Jeremy P. Tarcher, 1989.

Glover, Raymond F., ed. *The Hymnal 1982*. New York: Church Publishing Inc., 1985.

Henry, Earl. *Sight Singing*. Upper Saddle River, N.J.: Prentice Hall, 1997.

Herbert, George. "Love bade me welcome," from *The Oxford Book of English Verse 1250-1900*. A.T. Quiller-Couch, ed. Oxford: Clarendon, 1906, 295.

Hitchcock, H. Wiley. *Music in the United States: A Historical Introduction*. Upper Saddle River, N.J.: Prentice Hall, 1969 (revised, 2000).

Ottman, Robert W., and Frank D. Mainous. *Rudiments of Music.* Upper Saddle River, N.J.: Prentice Hall, 1995.

Perona-Wright, Leah, ed. "Voice for Life." Salisbury, U.K.: Royal School of Church Music, 2004.

Routley, Erik. *The Church and Music: An Enquiry into the History, the Nature, and the Scope of Christian Judgment on Music.* London: Gerald Duckworth and Co., 1950.

Sachs, Oliver. *Musicophilia.* New York: Alfred A. Knopf, 2007.

Schmeling, Paul. *Berklee Music Theory.* Boston: Berklee Press, 2005.

Schillibeeckx, Edward. *Jesus: an Experiment in Christology.* New York: Seabury, 1979.

Solzhenitsyn, Alexandr. "Lecture to the Swedish Academy," reprinted in *Nobel Lectures, Literature 1968–1980.* Sture Allén, ed. Singapore: World Scientific Publishing Co., 1993.

Westermeyer, Paul. *Te Deum: The Church and Music.* Minneapolis: Fortress Press, 1998.

Williams, Tennessee. *A Streetcar Named Desire.* New York: New Directions Books, 1947.

Periodicals

The American Organist. New York: American Guild of Organists.

Bishop, Randy. "How a Brazilian Tribe Learned to Sing to God." *Christianity Today International / Today's Christian* (formerly *Christian Reader*) 36, no. 4. July/August 1998.

The Choral Journal. Carroll Gonzo, ed. Oklahoma City, Okla.: American Choral Directors Association.

Popjes, Jack and Jo. "Music to Their Ears." *Mission Frontiers: The Bulletin of the U.S. Center for World Mission* 18. May–August 1996.

Reiter, Jerome P. *AAM Millenium Survey.* http://anglicanmusicians .org/id9.html. Little Rock, Ark: Association of Anglican Musicians, 2001.

Wyton, Alec "The Function of Music in Corporate Worship." *The Journal of Church Music.* December 1987.

Interviews, Correspondence, Internet Sources, and Lectures

Hustad, Donald P. Class lecture. Louisville, Ky.: Southern Seminary, School of Church Music, October 1975.

Iona: www.iona.org.uk.

Pulkingham, Betty Carr. Conversations, interviews, and e-mail correspondence between 1990 and 2008.

Rideout, Marti. Lectures at the Leadership Program for Musicians. Virginia Theological Seminary, Alexandria, Va., July 1995.

Roberts, William Bradley. Interviews and observations at the Taizé Community. Taizé, France, October 1992.

The Royal School of Church Music in America:http://www.rscm.com/about_us/index.php.

Schram, Judith. E-mail correspondence, November 2007, July and August 2008.

Published Music

Global Praise, vols. I, II, and III. New York: General Board of Global Ministries, 1996, 2000, 2004.

Hawn, Michael, ed. *Halle Halle: We Sing the World Around.* Dallas: Choristers Guild, 1999.

Hurd, David. *Love Bade Me Welcome.* Pittsburgh, Pa.: Selah Publishing Co.

Palestrina, Giovanni Pierluigi da. *Sicut cervus*, available in numerous editions from a wide variety of sources.

Vaughan Williams, Ralph. *Five Mystical Songs.* Boston: ECS Publishing Co.

Index